ONE MAN'S

AIRLINE

Larry Green

Outskirts Press, Inc.
Denver, Colorado

Outskirts Press, Inc.
http://www.outskirtspress.com

ISBN: 978-1-4327-0062-1

Outskirts Press and the "OP" logo are trademarks belonging to Outskirts Press, Inc.

PRINTED IN THE UNITED STATES OF AMERICA

It all started in 1948 and ended, for me, forty years later in 1988. Unfortunately it ended for every one else in 1991. I always loved working for EASTERN AIRLINES and I think it shows from the dedication I put into every job I had, as it was with most EASTERN employees.

Working for EASTERN was always a joy because of the people at EASTERN. The basic heart of EASTERN was the best. That is what brought us back from disaster a couple of times. We had some good executives and some bad, but the people of EASTERN worked well with the good ones and survived the bad ones. It was the basic heart of EASTERN that kept the good name of EASTERN alive and well in the minds of our customers and the travel agents. To this day every travel agent I meet tells me they still miss EASTERN, that EASTERN was the best.

Of course there were low spots where people were brought in who restructured all the jobs and moved personnel around without knowing their strengths or capabilities. But the heart of EASTERN survived that also. There were also low points when some of our people thought it was in their best interests to go on strike. We survived that also.

I started with EASTERN at La Guardia Airport in February 1948 right in the middle of the "SEASON". I quickly learned what over bookings and oversales were all about.

In those days we started as a courier - we met the passengers at the limousines coming from New York and escorted them to the waiting room. And what a waiting room! It was only 13/14 feet wide and about 40 feet long - no air conditioning and almost no heat in the Winter. Of course we loaded the passengers directly from the waiting room through a door that when opened the passengers were outside on the ramp exposed to all the elements, no jetways in those days.

On the other side of the waiting room there was a corridor that was covered but the opposite side was open so the whole area was cold in the Winter and hot in the Summer. There was no heat or air conditioning in the corridors. A very primitive arrangement. Today's customers would be horrified.

I need to describe LaGuardia airport for you in 1948. The terminal building was a large round three story round building. In the front was a automobile ramp to the second floor where the passengers were dropped off and entered the building where all the airline ticket counters were located. Once in the rotunda, on the left was Eastern Airlines, Colonial Airlines and American Airlines. Then there was a double door leading to the observation deck which was on top of the gate structure. Those were the days when you could talk to your friends as they walked out to the plane. With security nowadays you can't even see the airplane. On the other side was Northwest Airlines, Capital Air lines, United Airlines and American Overseas. Northeast Airlines was there somewhere also. There was a kiosk to the right of the door and a company called North American Airways worked out of there. On the left side was a kiosk with a Western Union desk.

LaGuardia field was constantly sinking. The airport was built on top of a garbage dump which was not sufficiently compacted. To protect the runway from high winds and tides they built a dike around the north side of the airport that fronted on the North River. There were four large hangars on each side of the terminal. When they were built the hangar floor was flush with the ramp outside. When I was there the ramp was four or five feet below the hangar floor, the hangars being set on pilings.

The ground floor front door of the terminal building was where the passengers went after arriving with their baggage for transportation to their home or to the city. On the opposite side at the back end was a passage that open to the gate area. The passengers either carried their own baggage from the gates to the front or had a Skycap take it for them. The gate area was a one story structure about ½ mile long, a corridor about 10 to 12 feet wide with the individual airline gates, waiting rooms and gate ticket counters on the runway side. The gates paralleled the main runway, 31/13, and you could see the planes take off from the waiting rooms. The observation deck was on top of this structure. On the terminal side of the gate area, opposite from the waiting rooms, were openings for the limousines and buses to drop off their passengers.

The airport was opened in 1938 or 1939. It was built on top of a garbage dump as I said. It was originally called North Beach Airport before renaming it La Guardia in honor of the Mayor of New York. The terminal building was constantly sinking and there was an opening around the base to make it an independent structure. In 1948 the terminal building was up on steel jacks. Every few months a crew came through with surveying instruments and jacked up one side or another a few inches. The observation deck was something else. If you stood at one end of the observation deck and looked to the other end it looked like a roller coaster. I talked to a man who worked on the construction of the buildings and he said when they started work they drove a couple of 60 foot pilings and the pilings disappeared into the muck. They ended up driving 90 foot pilings.

3

Since the airport was built on a garbage dump there were numerous rats and mice around. The agents in those days worked four weeks on day shift and four weeks on afternoon shift. Two or three times a year they would get stuck on the midnight shift. The first week you worked midnights you figured "it's not so bad", the second week it was "it's not so bad but I wouldn't want to work it all the time ", the third week "it looks as if this will never end" and the fourth week every thing was bad and you couldn't wait to get off.

Back to the mice. On midnights I used to brown bag it. When I ate my sandwich a little mouse used to come around I would put a small piece of the sandwich on the end of my fingers and the mouse would come right up and eat it. Real cute little guy.

One of the operations agents used to put out all the lights and open the door a crack and try to shoot the rats with an air pistol. On the back side of the airport there was an employees cafeteria which we called the greasy spoon. Outside, by their kitchen, were a number of garbage cans. Once we had a new employee named John (Wilson?) who was deathly afraid of rats. I told him to stay clear of the garbage cans as there were always rats in them. He said "you are kidding". I said come on out back and I'll show you. We were standing about 30 feet away from the cans and I picked up a rock and hit one of the cans. Three or four rats jumped out and started running. John never went out the back way again.

EASTERN had gates 12 and 14. Gate 12 loaded from the waiting room and gate 14 loaded from the double doors where they brought in the baggage from the planes. Colonial Airlines at gate 15 was the only airline beyond us. It was there I met Charley Buckland for the first time. He was station manager for Colonial Airlines. He came with Eastern when Eastern bought Colonial Airlines about 1956 to get the New

4

York to Bermuda route and the New York to Montreal route. The whole airport was a very crude operation but, hey, everything was just getting started in those days.

I started work for $160.00 a month, which gratefully was increased, after a few months to $200.00 when a general raise was given. The manager (chief agent in those days) was Wayne Brockman. He was a good boss, he cared about the passengers and the people who worked for him. We had three supervisors Joe Tully, Hank Hay and Eddie Perschback they were all good guys too. The station manager was Binks Matey(?) But I never saw much of him.

We had a number of employees who had been in the Air Force during World War II working at LaGuardia for Eastern. We had Hank Hay, Phil Stahlman, Tom Rylles, Eddie Perschback and Jim(?) Timmerman. Some had applied to be pilots for Eastern and eventually Phil Stahlman, Tom Rylles and Timmerman became pilots for Eastern. Hank went on to be traffic manager at Idlewild, Phil flew for a long time and retired as a pilot for Eastern, Tom became a captain for Eastern but he had a lot of personal trouble and Timmerman was killed landing a plane at Kennedy. This was the first identified instance of a wind sheer which smashed the plane into the ground on landing.

In those days the personnel at the airport were divided up into Traffic and Operations. The Traffic people handled anything pertaining to the customer and operations did the paper work. That meant the Traffic people handled the passenger loading and pulling the loading stairs around and the baggage had to be brought to and from the plane. The Traffic agent loaded the baggage carts and pulled them to the plane. From there the Union guys loaded the plane. We had to pull the stairs and carts by hand as there were no tractors for us then. The sky caps helped us move the stairs and bring the bags in from the planes. Oh the fun we had in

5

the Winter! Sliding all over and not being able to move the carts.

We also handled the lost and found. Fortunately we had a very nice lady named Irma who took care of it most of the time. But every once in a while one of us agents had to do the job. And it was a thankless task. I remember we misplaced Mike Wallace's bag and Wayne Brockman had to take care of him. Mike was a local celebrity in those days. He and his wife had a radio or TV show much like the talk shows we have today. It got settled eventually but Mike was a little hot under the collar.

One day we had a bag that was unclaimed and it hung around for a few days. Finally Irma open the bag to see if it had and identification inside and the bag was full of pot. We called the police and they staked the bag out but no one ever showed up for it and the police took it away.

And we never lost a bag with a plain wool sweater in it. Every lost bag had a cashmere sweater, the expansive kind. The descriptions of the contents of the baggage was a standing joke and when many were found there were some mighty embarrassed customers.

We knew a few of the pilots in those days also since we were all crammed into a small space. We had a couple of Jokers too. One captain, on a DC-3, used to pull a trick when ever he had a new flight attendant. The captain and first officer world go up and pre flight the ship then the captain would go off on the passenger stairs and tell the flight attendant (there was only one on a DC-3) not to take off without him. The baggage/cargo loading of a DC-3 where the largest space was just behind the pilots and last minute items were put in the rear cargo hole. To load the baggage there was a nose stand up to the cockpit door. The captain would run up the nose stand and get back into his seat. The first officer

6

would call the flight attendant on the phone and tell her to close up they were leaving. The attendant not knowing the captain was on board would protest that the captain said not to leave without him. The pilot would say the heck with him it was departure time and he was leaving, which he did. They kept the cockpit door locked all the way to Washington. When the plane stopped on the ramp the first thing up was always the nose stand, the captain would come down, run around to the stairs, all out of breath, and yell to the flight attendant "I told you not to leave without me!"

Another captain had a trick that consisted of a five inch long dowel with a short piece of string knotted through a hole on one end. He would come up to you and very quickly slip it on to the button hole of your uniform. The trick was to get it off without cutting the string. We had guys walking around with the dowel hanging down for three and four days until the captain came back. Oh course you could always cut the string but that cheating. Airline people rarely see the pilots any more.

The idea, when you were hired, was to learn from the supervisors and the older agents how to write tickets and tag bags when it wasn't busy. No formal training or time was allotted. After a few months we had a very busy night at the gate and an agent named Duke Waddel was working the counter and I was checking bags. Now Duke was a good guy, but a free spirit and didn't take direction very well. I think he had some money also because he used to eat in the main terminal restaurant frequently while most of us were brown bagging it. He used to have a few schnapps with his meals also.

Any way, it was after dinner, Duke was feeling good and screwed up a few things. Joe Tully said to me "can you do this job?". I didn't know what to say because I didn't want to hurt Duke. Needing an answer I said I guess I could and with that I was an agent.

I had another incident that involved Joe Tully one evening. When a break came in the schedule everyone took off and left me alone at the ticket counter in the waiting room. In came an elderly gentlemen dressed in civilian clothes and he was schnokered. He was a retired General somebody and wanted to get on a plane to Washington. I told him he was in no condition to fly and suggested he go and get some coffee. He got all het up and said he knew Rickenbacker personally and he would call him if we did not let him on the plane. I believed him and called Joe up in the office. Joe said he would call Captain Eddie himself and see what to do. After making the call Joe called back and said Captain Eddie said "let him call I'll take care of him". The General went out to call and when he came back he was very humble and asked, politely, if he had a couple of cups of coffee would we take him. When he came back he was in much better shape and we did take him.

We had another person who was really obnoxious and he worked for EASTERN. A Mr. E. Smythe Gambrell was a lawyer, a stock holder and a friend of Capt Eddie. Every time he came to the airport he would bust into the managers office, sit down at his desk, without asking, and start telephoning. He would wait to the last minute to hurry to the gate for his flight.

One day Hank Hay, who was manager then, was at the gate and he knew Gambrell was in his office. He said to us we are going to get that flight out on time. So when departure time came the door was closed and the flight was sent away right on time. Gambrell came to the gate about 2 minutes after that and asked Hank where the flight was. Hank said it was gone, Gambrell asked if it had taken off yet and Hank said he didn't think so and Gambrell said bring it back. Hank said no that was against company regulations and refused. Gambrell ranted and raved but the airplane took off without him. I don't know if Hank ever heard the consequences of it.

It seems Mr. Gambrell was not too well thought of in Washington either. A secretary (male) to one of the CAB board members told me once that his boss was all set to vote for Eastern on some route case until Mr. Gambrell got up and spoke and his board member changed his mind and voted against Eastern.

I had the job one Winter of standing at the gate of the Florida flights with a number counter. We were flying Connies (749) by then and that had 60 seats. When we got to 60 on the counter I closed the gate door and dealt with who was left. This was a very unpleasant task and I was reamed royally many a time.

And things surprise you - I was watching the loading of a Miami flight and it ended with one open seat. In the meanwhile a flight to Boston was loading I noticed passengers standing of the stairs and I'm wondering why they don't finish and get the plane out. Good reason, there was no more seats for the people standing on the stairs. That's like hitting below the belt., we worry about the Miami flight and they oversell a Boston trip.

Working at the airport was stimulating because you met lots of people. I was introduced to Elizabeth Taylor, she was 17 or 18 years old at the time, and she was truly a beautiful girl. Another time I was escorted Veronica Lake to the gate for an early boarding. We were walking along the corridor and no one else was around except a kind of creepy little guy seem to be following us. I asked Ms. Lake if she knew who he was and she said oh yes "That's my husband Andre de Toth". Fortunately I had not used any adjectives to describe him. I brought him up so he could walk with us.

9

In removing oversales, I once had to <u>ask</u> Primo Canera, the boxer, to leave the plane. When he started standing up I thought he would never quit, he was at least a foot taller than I. If he had refused I would have just said "thank you have a nice flight". Fortunately he was a nice man and followed me off the plane.

I had one case of too much celebrity notoriety. There was a TV show which had a basset hound named Morgan. He was most popular. Obviously the owners, whose name I can't remember, thought they were big shots too. When they checked in at the up stairs ticket counter it was late. Then they said they were going up stairs to the bar on the third floor for a drink, to which I advised them they did not have enough time. They went anyway. I was down at the gate when the 11:59pm flight to Miami departed. They came up just as the plane was leaving the ground (which you could see from where we were standing.) They demanded to know where flight 631 was I turned and pointed and said "there it goes" as it flew by. They demanded I bring the flight back. I told them I didn't have the authority to do that. Then it was "who does" "only the station manager" "where is he" "home in bed" "call him and get him up" "no sir, I am not going to do that". They went away mad and I never heard of them or the dog again. He never knew about it but I hope Frank Stulgaitis, the station manager, appreciates his full night sleep that night.

Speaking of Frank he had one chore he loved to do. In those days the Connie (L749) had a "speed pack" which attached to the bottom of the airplane. It could carry a large load, I think 8 tons but that is a guess. In the Winter Frank would take a speed pack up state in New York and fill it with snow. Eastern then flew it to San Juan and unloaded the snow in Munoz Rivera Park for the kids to play in, eat ice cones and throw snow balls. We did that for a number of years.

Just to show how much things change- I was working at the gate one afternoon and a husband and wife came running up carrying their bags. They were going on the flight which already had pulled the stairs. I started to hustle them out to the airplane and the husband stopped me and asked me to take care of his car which he had left at the entrance to the terminal. I said I would park it and leave him a message and the keys in the Will Call as to where the car was parked for when he came back. I asked for the keys and he said they were in the car. He made the plane and I hurried up to the front of the terminal. There was his car with the door open and WITH the engine running. Today the car would be gone.

The airports were very "loose" in those days. Late in the evening when American had no flights left for the day one of their counter personnel would use the loud speaker system to announce the NOON BALLOON TO RANGOON. I think the man would used to do that was Frank Sweeney. And who could forget Northeast Airlines page for a Tondalao Schwartz and a Mrs. Schwartz, who didn't think it was very funny, chewing out the Northeast agent. Now that WAS funny.

The DC-3 was easy to work. A case in point- Bill Fealy, the operations man, came to me one day and told me the flight to Boston was running an hour late and he wanted to make up time by turning the flight really quick. He had the captain stop number 1 engine (the left one on the side toward the gates) but kept number 2 engine going, we hustled the passengers on to the plane, put what little baggage in the tail compartment and took less than two minutes on the gate. We made up so much time the flight arrived in Boston only about 15 minutes late. The passengers were probably wondering what was going on. Bill was about my age but had pure white hair. He said it turned white when he was 21. Anyway it made him look older and the company made him an operations supervisor. Besides that he was very good and knew his stuff.

When I was first with EASTERN the DC-3 had to have a set of stairs (4 or 5 steps) rolled up to load and unload passengers. After a while all the DC-3s were reworked to have a built-in set of stairs on the loading door. The door was hinged on the bottom and a set of chains on each side kept the stairs in place as the passengers used them. This made it very easy to close up the door quickly and get the plane ready. The DC-3 also had safety pins in the landing gear to keep the wheels from being retracted on the ground. The last thing the operations agent did before sending the plane off was to pull the pins, place them on the ground at his feet so the captain could see that the pins were out and then signal the plane out. One afternoon the agent forgot to pull the pins and the captain took off with the pins still in place. We found out about when there was a lot of noise on the radio, the captain was blowing his top, he had to land and come back to have the pins taken out. I don't remember what happened to the agent. The DC-3 also had a tail board put in place in windy weather to keep the rudder from blowing in the wind.

My first flight ever was not until 1949. We had scheduled a DC-4 to fly a group of crippled children around New York. I was working at the departure desk in operations area and the captain asked if I had ever flown. I said no and he said come and go on the fly around. There were no seats so they put me in the jump seat. On the DC-4 is was really a jump seat. It was a padded board that folded down between the two pilots seats, my feet were almost in the instruments. We had to pass right by the tower on take off so the captain said for me to duck down so they could not see me as I was not supposed to be there. It was a beautiful ride around New York City and the kids really enjoyed it.

My first real flight, going some where, was from La Guardia to San Juan, Puerto Rico. We had just inaugurated a new route and the company wanted us to see San Juan. They gave us two days at the Caribe Hilton, which was also new at the time. One of our guys didn't make it back in two days, the excuse - he got hit in the head by a coconut, yeah it was a coconut drink called Coco Loco. I enjoyed the trip very much and subsequently in my time with Eastern made about 50 flights to San Juan. I guess I have a little Puerto Rican blood in me I love the island and the people.

To show you how slow flights were in those days let me tell you about flight 571 which left La Guardia at about 11:00pm every night. It went nonstop to Washington and then stopped at every station all the way ro San Antonio. In the morning we had a DC-4 that went non stop to Houston and people going to San Antonio flew it to Houston and made a connection with 571 in Houston to San antonio.

The idea of "coach" flights started while I was at La Guardia. Up until that time all the flights were first class and one price at that. There were excursion fares from time to time in the slow seasons. The coach flights started as night coaches, to utilize the planes at night when not many people would fly. The price was half to two thirds off the first class fares.

The idea was to get more utilization out of the airplane. If it sat at the airport all night it was not making any money. This was particularly true for north/south routes. The companies flying east/west could fly over night between the east coast to the west coast at the regular fares.

Capital Airways started the first coach flights. Then the rest of the industry jumped on the band wagon. Checking in the first of the coach flights on Eastern was a hoot- as mothers brought the kids out in pajamas and robes. I guess they thought it was like a berth on a train.

Speaking of Capital Airlines many airlines were starting to replace the DC-4s with DC-6s. Capital could not afford the new planes and figured the only way most people could tell a DC-4 from a DC-6 was that the DC-4 had round windows and the DC-6 square windows. So Capital Airlines painted the outside of the plane to make the windows look square - instant DC-6. Capital was eventually folded into United Airlines.

Coach flights lasted only a short time as night coaches then airlines started flying coaches in the daytime. The night coach was still the least expensive of all flights. In the daytime a whole plane was classified as coach. First class was on separate, usually newer, planes. It wasn't until Delta had difficulty in keeping up with the number of planes needed to operate that way that the two classes were combined on to one plane.

The night coaches lasted until the jets came in and for a little while after that but the timing was all wrong for jets. If you left New York for Miami at 11:59PM you got into Miami at 2:30AM and the same when you went back to New York. No one wanted to arrive at 2:30AM. Relatives and friends were reluctant to pick up a passenger at those times and even cabs were hard to find. That coupled with the crazy ticket pricing where the day flights were as cheap as the night flights cut out the night coach as they were. The airlines with east-west routes continued to fly the night flights because of the length of the flight and they are now called the RED EYE flights.

La Guardia was right on the what they call the North River. The place was hot in the Summer and very cold in Winter with winds whistling across the water. Some of the guys would come in from the ramp with ice covered eye brows.

Leaving late at night (12:30-1:00am) in the Winter was a

really chore. We had freezing fog sometimes. You would start the car, turn on the heater and go scrape the windshield, then scrape it again because it would freeze right up again. It was not until the heater got car hot enough that you could keep it clear with the windshield wipers.

The Fall was fun also, with the winds and tide hammering on the dike. In one storm the water came over the dike and flooded the field also the parking lot down by the Eastern hangar. All the employees cars parked there were ruined by water up to the door handles.

Idlewild, (Kennedy) airport was open (1950) but only one domestic airline, National, flew there. All the International airlines used this new facility including Pan American. Up to that time French was the diplomatic language of the World and almost any language could be used by the pilots. About the time Idlewild opened the official language for all the airlines was designated to be English. The Air France pilots refused to speak English and called in French until the tower people refused to answer. Pan Am had used the Marine Terminal at La Guardia up until that time. They had a good employees cafeteria over there where we would go to eat if we had time. Another good place to eat was in United' s hanger where there was also an employees cafeteria.

National, who was supposed to be flying in to Idlewild, did not fly for quite a while due to a pilot strike. Then National hired new pilots and resumed flying. When the strike was over and the regular pilots came back, George Baker, president of National, refused to let the new pilots go and kept both on the payroll. It was told to me by National people that when a regular pilot and the new hirer were captain and first officer they did not even talk to each other. That lasted for years and got even worse when Pan Am merged National into Pan Am.

15

Before Eastern moved to Idlewild we used to rent the Pan American planes in the Winter to fly passengers to Miami. Pan American's main maintenance bases was in Miami and they used to deadhead the planes to Miami so it was a win win situation for both of us. Pan American pilots would fly the plane but the cabin crew were Eastern flight attendants. The people who really made out were the Eastern pilots. Because of union rules if it was an Eastern passenger flight they had to be paid for it. Since it was a Pan American plane their pilots had to fly it.

The Eastern pilots were assigned by crew schedule according to their bid sheets. This led to the real "GHOST RIDERS IN THE SKY". Pilots who flew to Miami and back and never left the ground. (And got paid for it)

Eastern would send the traffic and operations agents to Idlewild to work the flights. We would take our own baggage tags and tickets with us. On one occasion we had a wire from Miami that one of the passengers bags was missing. We, and the Pan Am people, search all over for the bag and could not find it. With only one plane and our own baggage tags how could the bag be missing? Three days later we received a wire from BOAC "we have one of your bags here at Heathrow, would you like to have it?"

We had a few accidents at La Guardia while I was there. Fortunately no one died. American Airlines landed a Convair wheels up. The captain did a beautiful job- he didn't even scratch the wings, it was a perfect wheels up landing. Northeast had Convair that landed perfectly also, only it was parallel to the runway and unfortunately 30 yards in to the North River. It landed on the water and the tail stuck up out of the water form 3 or 4 days. All the passengers got off OK. The funniest one, because no one was hurt, was a Pan American L-649 cargo plane that landed on runway 31 but skidded off into the water. It was right opposite to were I was working but 400 yards away, I started running toward the plane and before I got half way there a Pan American maintenance truck reached the ship and was painting the name out on the tail. I figured they didn't need me and I returned to the gate.

There was one accident on the ramp in the TWA area. One of the ramp men walked in to a moving propeller of a TWA plane. He was killed instantly.

We had various sales campaigns that involved the ticket counter such as the SMILE campaign. We were told to smile at the customers and Eastern had little cards printed with the word SMILE on them. One day Jack Carley was handing a customer who had a problem. Jack offered him assistance and smiled at him and the customer blew up saying "what are you grinning at you stupid jackass!". Hank Hay (supervisor) was standing near by and Jack turned to him and said "you see doesn't always work" (the smile).

One New Years Day, I was lucky (?) enough to be the supervisor on the early morning shift. We had many passengers check-in and sent to the gate. It was very foggy but the planes were leaving the gate. After a few hours we found that the planes were all on the ground waiting for take off. Then they began returning to the gate and canceling. We worked like dogs to get them all taken care of. Just after we finished the large crowd I had a call from Col. Frost. (This man was amazing for his recall of names, I think he knew the name of everyone who worked for EASTERN.) Col Frost was a Vice President for EASTERN and I believe Captain Eddies brother in law. He asked if we need any help at the airport and I wanted to say not now but we sure could have used it a couple of hours ago. However I just said no it was all over but thank you very much.

Maybe one of the reasons we didn't have much trouble on

that day was the fact we came to work right from a New Years Eve party. Two of our female agents still had on their evening clothes and they looked great. They didn't have any problems with any customers.

Along about 1951 I was sent to St Louis for an interview for the ticket counter manager in St Louis. Clunet Lewis was the sales manager. We had a nice interview and Clunet said I was the man he wanted. All he could offer in salary increase was $30.00 a month. This meant I would have to sell my house and pick up everything and move to St Louis for $30.00 more a month. I told him I wanted the job but I could not do it for $30.00 a month. So that ended that venture.

Back in those days there was no overtime or shift differential. If you worked overtime you sometimes got time off. We had a problem one night with the airport closing down due to fog. We had to take care of the people who had their flights cancel. I had a line of about 10 people in front of me and proceeded to handle them one at a time. My shift ended at midnight and it was now about 12:30am. The second man in line started to give me a hard time. I stopped and said loud enough for the whole line to hear. "Sir, my shift ended at midnight and I do not get paid overtime, if do don't want me to help you I will gladly close up and go home." The rest of the line was on my side and told him to take what was offered and leave.

In 1952 the Newark airport had a series of bad accidents happen. First a non sked crashed in Elizabeth and killed all the passengers. Then American Airlines crashed and killed all the passengers including former Secretary of War Robert Patterson. But the crushing blow was a National Airlines plane that took the top off an apartment building, also killing all on board and some in the building. There had been protests about the safety of the field and with that crash Newark airport was closed for about a year while they built a new runway.

This naturally caused major problems at La Guardia.

On the first day of the closure EASTERN sent some of our people over to Idlewild and we ran some flights out of there. At that time we had just received the new Super Connies-1049s and we were told they couldn't land at La Guardia, they had been using Newark. I had a couple of passengers who came up to me at La Guardia and were booked on a flight to Miami on a Super Connie flight. I stuffed them into a cab and sent them to Idlewild. Ten minutes later our Super Connie pulled up on the ramp at La Guardia.

In 1952 I transferred to Idlewild (now Kennedy Airport) as chief agent to help start up the new operation over there. Hank Hay was the Traffic Manager and Jim Riordan was the assistant manager. We had very little space and negotiations started immediately for a larger area. As chief agent I had Wednesdays and Thursdays off for years. Jim Riordan had Mondays and Tuesdays off and we both worked on Fridays, Saturdays and Sundays, which were our busiest days.

We didn't have a big contingent of people working there and the schedule was for one hour for dinner. I was in charge one evening when Colonel Frost came through. There was only one agent on the counter. Colonel Frost got me and said "Larry, where are all the agents?" I said they were eating. And he said why are they so long and I told him they had one hour eating schedules. He said get them back here and change the schedules. I got them back in a hurry. When I told Hank Hay I was given the job of working out the schedule for everyone from then on. And I worked out some beauties.

One schedule I worked out changed days off every week until the fourth week when the new schedule came out.

When the new schedule came out two to four agents ended with two days off and started with two days off giving them four days in a row off to go some place. I would work up two or three schedules but always asked the agents to vote on which one they wanted.

In the Summer Captain Eddie had his junior staff meetings. Hank as manager was "invited" to go. As I said in those days we flew the Constellations as first class flights. In the summer there were very few customers going to Miami first class. The company business class passes allowed employees to fly first class but no people with vacation passes. On the day Hank left for Miami there was no customers on board just the pass riders going to the meeting. The pilot knew Hank had flown a B-17 in WW II and asked if he would like fly the plane for a while. Hank was delighted to have the opportunity and took the wheel. Now the Constellation had trim tabs which had to be adjusted to fly the plane straight and smooth. Hank did that OK until the wise guys in the back decided to harass him. They waited until he had the tabs set then altogether walked to the very rear of the plane. As soon as Hank had the tabs set again they would all walk to the very front. And so on.

Hank was a real good guy however when the first break in the traffic came for coffee on the morning shift Hank's first words were "are you buying?" He was always trying to get someone to buy him coffee. Hank had money and if he thought you could not afford it he would always pick up the check. Hank never cashed his Eastern checks. He had to send them to the bank to prove he was still working and then received a allowance from a trust fund his father left him. When he went away he told me to just sign his checks and send them into the bank.

Idlewild airport was always a mess in the early days. The buildings were all Quonset huts. Once you left the gate you had to find your way thru a maze of chain pathways to your proper airplane. The opportunities to get on the wrong airplane were numerous. We had a lady we checked in one day to Danville, Va. (yes we actually flew there). She left the gate OK and on time. Forty minutes later she was back at the ticket counter. I asked what happened and she said as they were taxing to the runway she noticed everyone was speaking Spanish. She called a flight attendant and found she was on Avianca non-stop to Bogota. They had to bring her back to the terminal.

As we did before we continued to rent the Pan AM planes in the Winter to fly passengers to Miami. We never knew until the last minute how many seats we would have on their airplanes. They also had 2 or 3 different configurations for each plane, we were told the day of the flight the actual number of seats. One night it was freezing cold with sleet and we decided to board the plane in the Pan Am hanger. We rented a Carey bus to take the passengers to the hanger. We checked all the passengers in at the Eastern ticket counter and only bussed the correct number of passengers for the number of seats we had. We loaded the plane and I was checking it out and found two passengers standing in the aisle. We went hunting for the two empty seats and could find none, then I counted the seats and found we were two short of the number they told us. I told the Pan Am captain and he said "no problem". He got hold of the Pan Am maintenance man and had them bring in two seats and bolt them to the floor. Weird but true.

Another happening with the Pan Am rentals was when we rented a Boeing Stratocruiser. This was a double decked airplane. It was used mostly for long international flights and the downstairs was a beautiful lounge with a bar. The international airlines didn't sell these seats but when Eastern rented them we sold those seats (7) also since the flight was only four hours to Miami. One night we had an Arab, who by the time he boarded found all the seats in the main cabin full. There was a seat in the lounge (which we thought of as a deluxe seat since it was bigger than the seats above). He steadfastly refused to be seated in the "basement". I tried to convince him it was a deluxe seat but he said no! Fortunately we had another flight to Miami 45 minutes later and I put him on that.

In the Winter the flights to Miami were always sold out and we has a standby list to accommodate passengers who wanted to wait and see if there were any "no shows". We would list the passengers in the order they came to the counter. It was a tough position and some times I would work it on particularly busy days. The first thing you did was to dump the tickets and contents from the ticket envelope on the ticket counter in plain sight of all. Often there was money in there meant as a bribe to move them up on the list. I would just say politely "you left some money in your envelope" and for them to pick it up. Once a man, who had been at the standby position, followed me into the Brass Rail restaurant as I was going to eat. He approached and said "if I give you $50.00 would that help?" I said "you give me $50..00 and I'll make sure you don't get on the airplane, OK?". He looked at me for a few minutes, then said "Oh, I get it, forget I said anything."

The night shift at Idlewild was always an adventure.

In the fifties most of our Puerto Rican travelers were very unsophisticated and scared to death of flying. (with good reason there were a number of Puerto Rican people killed by airlines crashing into the Atlantic soon after taking off from San Juan, none of them EASTERN.). Some of our passengers sought courage from a bottle and some got a little worse for wear. One night two men were dragging a third man between them to the gate. I asked where they were going. They said pointing to the man in the middle "he go Puerto

Rico". I said not tonight fellows bring him back tomorrow when he can walk by himself.

Another night a man caused a disturbance at the gate. He was under the influence and hit our operations agent with a walking stick. The police were called and he was arrested. Since I was the supervisor the police insisted I be in court the next morning to press charges. When the case was called the Judge asked him if he wanted a lawyer and he said yes. The judge called the bailiff over and spoke quietly to him. Then the bailiff came over to me and asked if I really want the man in jail. I said no I didn't want him to go to jail if it could be worked out. Then the bailiff (the judge instructed him) went over to the man and talked to him. He said to the man "all you really want to do is to get to Puerto Rico is that right?" the man nodded and the bailiff said "if you ask for a lawyer you will be delayed for a week or two however if you pleaded guilty the Judge will release you if you promise to get on the plane and return to Puerto Rico". The man said OK and we went up to the Judge who looked at me and said "can you get him out tonight"? I said I could if he behaved himself. That finished the court case. When I went in that afternoon the man was sitting on a little green bench outside the Brass Rail just across from our ticket counter. I asked him to stay there and I would come and get him and take him to the plane. He never moved until I came to get him. That worked out fine. (or without a fine).

In the fifties we were operating DC 4s on the coach flights to Puerto Rico. This was a long flight and required max gas on board. When the weather was bad they had to fly the "Romeo" route which was a stop in Charleston, SC for fuel.

Eastern configured the plane with 68 seats, however we could not fill them all on such a long flight to Puerto Rico as we had max gas and the gas weighed too much. We could get on maybe 52 or 53. Someone came up with the idea that the Puerto Ricans were smaller and weighed less than their Stateside compatriots.

In those days airplanes (all piston engined) had a critical weight that they could carry. Passengers were figured at 160 pounds in the Summer and 165 pounds in the Winter. The actual weight was used for baggage and all cargo and gas on board. The DC 4 also had to be loaded correctly in the belly bins. After landing and parking at the gate a tail fork had to be attached to the rear end of the plane so if too much weight was in the rear end the tail would not hit the ground. Naturally if the tail fork rested on the ground the weight had to be redistributed before it left the gate.

Any way the idea was to take an adding machine to the gate and ask every passenger their weight. That worked out well and we could get about 58 to 60 passengers on board. Now we all had picked up a bit of Spanglish so we could record the proper weights when given to us in Spanish. One evening I was at the door asking for the weights. We would ask the question "how much do you weigh" and for those who did not know what we said we asked "Cuanto Pesa ?". Naturally the answers were in English and Spanish. The frequent Spanish answer was "Ciento veintisinco" which is 125 pounds. Which was about right for those going thru. This particular evening we had a number of Spanish only speakers. The first one said "Ciento veintisinco" and I guess the next passengers in line thought this was the pass word as they all said "Ciento veintisinco" until a man 6 feet tall and about 200 pounds gave me the same answer. I stopped him and said wait a minute you don't weigh 125 pounds. The passengers around us, speaking Spanish, got the correct weight from him.

We also found Pan Am could get more passengers on their DC4s than we could. Someone found out that while Eastern was using 6 pounds per gallon of gas Pan Am was using 5.6

24

pounds. So now we got a few more on the plane.

At this point Pan Am was the only competitor to San Juan. When anyone called in for a flight to San Juan on Pan Am they were confirmed. They confirmed everybody. Then Pan Am went and got whatever number of airplanes they needed. They used DC-4s and probably had a number of them which could no longer be used on International flights. Years later I met the man who devised this system- Carlos DeGabriel who owned Superior Travel in Miami Beach when I knew him.

At night we could hear on the loud speaker system announcing flight 215 to San Juan, then 215B, 215C, 215D, 215E. Of course they all had different gates and it was very confusing to their passengers since there was no jetways only chained walks which could lead to any number of airplanes. This gave rise to that which has become a joke in the industry (if anyone jokes anymore) but it really happened. A passenger by the name of Martinez went out the gate to go to San Juan, boarded the plane and took off. Once aloft the Stewardess asked if he wanted a Manhattan or Martini, not speaking much English he said "Si Martinez", meaning, yes he was Martinez. So the stewardess brought him the Martini. After a couple strong Martinis he went to sleep and when the plane landed he got off. He couldn't figure how Puerto Rico got so cold. He was on a flight to Europe and they had landed in Gander for fuel. Naturally Pan Am got him back to San Juan albeit a few days late.

In the fifties all the International flights from Europe to New York landed in Gander to refuel. Once or twice all the airports on the East coast where shut down due to fog. The airports from Boston thru Washington where closed for two or three days. This meant all the International flights were stuck in Gander. There was one small hotel which quickly filled up and then all the other passengers had to make due on the cold airplanes. When the jets came in that was the end of the hay day at Gander.

As I said the night shift was always an adventure. When the weather was bad the day shift could always go home and let the afternoon shift handle the problems but the night shift had to stay until we got all the airplanes out or we canceled the flight.

One night we had a flight to Miami which loaded on time and left the gate on time but by the time it got to the runway the wings were iced up. So they sent the airplane to the hanger to glycol the wings and sent it back to the gate for dispatch. The plane went to the runway again and again it was iced up. They followed the same procedure with the same results. Now the captain, back in the hanger, had the wings sprayed for the third time and called the tower for clearance from the hanger. He got the clearance, roared out of the hanger straight to the runway and took off.

On another night a coach flight to San Juan took multiple delays and the passengers became unruly. They started throwing things at the agents. So I cleared the ticket counter and called the Port Authority police to come. The policeman who came was not much help. He blamed us for not getting the flight out on time. We finally got the 11:30 flight out at 5:30am.

At this time we were flying Lockheed Constellation L749s, 1049s, DC-4s, DC-3s and Martin 404s. The Constellations were operated as first class flights. Pass riders were not allowed to fly on the first class Constellations. I guess I helped break that restriction. We had a busy period, particularly to Miami, and we had pass riders standing by for the coach flights some for as long as three days. On the fourth day I stuck a bunch of pass riders on the Constellation, which had only 11 passengers booked on it and the coach flights were still full.

The next day I was talking to someone in the Home Office and they told me "can you imagine someone put a bunch of pass riders on the Connie". I said "is that so, what do you know". It also helped that Mrs. Armstrong, the presidents wife, was in Miami watching the pass riders standing by down there and not getting on and I think she got the restriction lifted.

When we first started at Idlewild there was no seat assignments. Naturally everybody crowded up to the doors to be first on the plane and get the seat they wanted. One of the tricks to get on first was to claim they needed a wheelchair. We had to go along with it. We used to take the wheelchairs out a different gate from where the airplane was loading. Remember the customers had to walk across the tarmac and climb the stairs to get in the plane. One day I was pushing a woman out of the other gate. I told the operations agent to hold up loading until I got the woman on the airplane but he forgot. When she saw the passengers going across the tarmac toward the stairs she jumped out of the wheelchair and beat the first passengers up the stairs. I was quite hot under the collar.

One night we had a mechanical delay on an airplane and the mechanics were fixing it on the ramp. It was freezing cold and our mechanic could hardly hold a wrench or a screwdriver. The customers were not too happy and one man was particularly obnoxious. I went out to see how things were going and the mechanic was still on a tall ladder, with a freezing wind blowing, working on the engine. When I came back in Mr. Obnoxious got me again. I tried to mollify him but he wouldn't quit so I offered to take him outside and he and I would stand there and watch the mechanic as he worked. He refused and walked away and was I glad as it was DAMN cold outside.

In 1954(?) we received a great new airplane, which we

called the DC7B the *Golden Falcon*. A friend of Captain Eddie's, Harley Earl of General Motors, designed the inside of the plane. He said he was just waiting for a plane big enough to do a great design job. It was a beautiful airplane, the decor inside was new, different and beautiful and the turbocompound engines made the plane the fastest in the fleet. Instead of four hours to Miami it was 3 1/2 hours.

When it was introduced the Company had fly arounds New York from Idlewild. Frank Maddox from the home office was in charge of filling the seats for these trips. I asked if we could get any for other airline people working at Idlewild. He said he was sorry but all the seats were booked for commercial accounts and travel agents.

It just so happened that the first couple of flights had a big no show problem. Frank came to me and asked if I could help fill some of the seats if the problem continued. I said I thought we could do it. (In those days I knew people at just about every airline at the airport.) I made up a bunch of lists and had people standing by for every flight after that. We made a lot of friends for the DC7B and Eastern on those two days.

About 1953 we moved to the end of the terminal into a new bigger area. The operations was upstairs and we had a VIP room also. The VIP room was a Captain Eddie version- very sparse with not too comfortable furniture. But we did manage to take a number of VIPs up there.

This new facility was near the customs exit so we had first crack at passengers looking to go beyond New York. We had three international agents assigned to "work the customs" for new passengers. They made friends with other airline people from the international airlines who were assigned in customs to assist their inbound passengers. Naturally they would call our agents over to handle the onward journey.

We had Johnny George and Frank Rivera. (can't remember the other agents name).

They had me take Gene Kelly to the VIP room, having just come from London. He was a very nice man but very tired all he wanted to do was rest, where no one would hound him.

When the Arthur Godfrey show was on TV they usually flew with Eastern. Whenever Godfrey would fly he had Dick Merrill fly the plane. We flew the McGuire sisters Dorothy, Phyllis and Christine on many of their trips. Dorothy and Christine were always on time and we took them up to the VIP room. Phyllis was always late and we had to run her to the plane. One neat thing was about their baggage. Each one had about five pieces they were all the same style and color, so to tell which bag belonged to which girl the eight corners on each bag were color coded. One girls bags had all green corners, another one red and the third one blue.

I got to meet Gloria DeHaven at Idlewild and messed her up. She was going with Dick Fincher (he was an Oldsmobile dealer in Miami) at the time and she accompanied him to the airport where he was to take the flight to Miami. She got me to one side and asked me to get her on the plane at the last minute as a surprise to Fincher. I said sure. I would watch the plane and get her on at the last minute. So I kept checking the plane and now it was late (I thought). I went up to operations to find out when it would leave and was told it had already left. They had switched gates and I was watching the flight to San Juan. Now I had to, very sheepishly, tell Miss DeHaven how I messed up. She was very nice about it and I had a solution for her. The plane Fincher was on was a Connie (left at 11:59PM) and we had a DC-7 leaving at 12:30AM. I explained the DC-7 was faster and she might catch him in the baggage area. The next time I saw her she said she did catch him in the terminal. They were later married so I guess it worked out OK.

The Station Manager at Idlewild in those days was Johnny Mitchell and he was a good guy. Of course I have seen him burn (quietly) when someone pulled a stupid goof. I had a debate with him one time which worked out OK. We had a flight from Miami, 658, which was a constellation from Miami to New York and then had a change of gage to a Martin 404 from New York to Boston. On this particular day 658 was running an hour late and Johnny was talking about getting the "Idlewild section" out on time. I objected on the grounds that it was sold as a thru flight and the customers would be pissed if the "section" left without them. Furthermore we had only 8 passengers boarding in Idlewild and there were 32 thru passengers. Of course he was the boss and if he said go, it would. We argued for a while and I remember threatening him with going out and sitting on the nose wheel to keep it from going. (this referred to a passenger who was oversold at Newark the year before and DID go sit on the nose wheel. It made the front page of the Daily News.) Anyway he finally gave in and held the "Idlewild section."

One day we had J Fred Muggs (a chimpanzee TV celebrity) and his owner going out on a flight. The New York office had arranged for them to sit in the regular seats in the cabin. J Fred Muggs was all dressed in shirt, tie, coat and pants and was wearing saddle shoes. I sat them in Hank's office to wait for the flight. The chimp sat in Hank's office chair and pulled the arm right off. He was one strong little sucker. When it came time to board I took them out early to the airplane. Mr. Muggs walked along holding his owners hand plopping one foot after the other and as we were making it across the tarmac Captain Eddie came along and said to me "we'll doing anything to get a customer won't we."

We had various altercations with passengers at Idlewild. One afternoon the counter was very busy, the weather was lousy the customers were short tempered. One of our female agents was taking care of a man and I guess he was not getting what he wanted and started to cuss a the agent using very ungentlemanly words. I was working front of counter and told him he could either refrain from using that kind of language or leave the counter. Then I had to go upstairs to operations to see when things would straighten out. This was an internal steel staircase with a steel door at the bottom. Halfway up the stairs I heard the door open and close and up the stairs came the customer. I remember thinking if he came for a fight I would kick him right down the stairs. Thank God, it turned out he realized what a jerk he made out of himself came to apologize, which I gladly accepted.

Another altercation came one night when a passenger walked up to the counter. Frank Rivera was behind the counter and asked if he could help the man. The man said to Frank "I don't want any help from you, you xxxx$#@." Now Frank was a real gentleman and never used cuss words and it was as if the man had slapped him across the face. Frank was a loss for words. I was standing nearby working front of the counter, and realized the man was drunk. I stepped in and said to Frank "don't worry about it Frank he's not going anywhere tonight". The man, he was a big nasty drunk about 50, grabbed me by the shirt at the shoulder and started rocking me back and forth saying "what do you mean I'm not going anywhere." I said "that is just what I said- you are not going anywhere tonight". With that he ripped the whole arm out of the shirt. I guess I got a little hot and wheeled around and hit him with a left punch that knock his hat off and staggered him back. Then he made a mistake he tried to kick me in the groin and I reached down and caught the foot so now he was dancing around on one foot. The baggage room was right behind the ticket counter and the door was open, over the counter jumped two of our baggage men and grabbed the man. Which was a good thing for me as I was going to flip the leg in the air and dump

31

him on his back, I could have had real trouble if he split his head open. We called the police and they took him away - never heard much about it after that.

We started getting part of some Mexico City business while I was at Idlewild. Wayne Brockman had left Eastern and was now station manager for Air France. Strange as it may seems Air France had the only non stop from New York to Mexico City. The flight was very popular both from Paris and from New York.

Air France was allowed to carry USA passengers from New York to Mexico City under the airlines fifth freedom rights. Unfortunately for Wayne, Paris used to oversell the flight frequently. Wayne would come to us and get seats from New York to Miami and then an airline called Guest Airways would take them to Mexico City on an old DC-4, a real long flight at their speed.

American Airlines had a flight from New York to Mexico City that stopped in Dallas but at that time they were not operating out of Idlewild. The United States and Mexico did not have an airline agreement at that time. In about 1946 American was granted the route from Dallas to Mexico City, Pan Am was given the Brownsville to Mexico City and Eastern was given the New Orleans to Mexico City. The Civil Aeronautics Board, which granted these routes, asked the airlines not to make any private deals with the Mexico government. Eastern abided with this request and listed the route on our schedules for about ten years as a dormant route. American and Pan Am did not follow directions and made private deals with the Mexican government so they were flying into Mexico City in the early 1950's. When a new agreement was made with the Mexican Government, about 1958, it included a non stop route from New York to Mexico CityEastern was awarded the route and American and Pan Am put up a howl. The CAB's answer was that they

32

did not follow the CAB's request therefore Eastern gets the route. In order to get the Mexican government to allow us to land in Mexico City we had to give Aero Mexico one of our DC-8s (they paid us for it). They had no equipment to fly the recipical route.

The Union guys, both the ramp service men and the mechanics, and I were good friends and we always got along well at Idlewild. I could go in and look for baggage and take it out at any time unless there was a "job action" going on. Then they would tell me "Larry don't not touch anything today" and said "yes sir" and just turned around and walk out.

Eastern had some of the best mechanics in the business. We had one line chief, name of Churchy, who could stand on the tarmac as a plane was coming in and tell what was the matter with the engines. And it would be fixed right away. We never worried when he was on duty. Churchy went on to become a flight engineer, and we lost him in the strike when the FAA decreed all flight engineers had to become pilots and our union refused to do so.

We had another guy by the name of Brown who was acting line chief on some days. He was a Union rabble rouser. We always worried when he was on, as he couldn't fix anything.

After I moved to Miami I had a small apartment hotel. Some on the mechanics from Idlewild came and stayed with me and I put them up for free. One I remember was Red Cavenaugh and his family.

Funny things happen at the airports too. One night a lady checked in for a flight to Miami and then asked if anyone needed a car. We all looked at each other and one agent said yes he did so she have him the keys, registration and the parking ticket and got on the plane. It was legitimate alright and he drove it for at least a year.

Another day a family ran up to the ticket counter and said they had stopped for lunch and someone had stolen their baggage from the trunk of their rented car while they were eating. They did not discover this until they went to give the baggage to the sky cap. About that time we had a call from reservations telling us the restaurant had called and what happened was another of their customers discovered someone had taken his rented car. It turns out the two cars were identical and the keys from the first car worked in the second and our customer had driven off in the wrong car.

I was chief agent of a team with Tommy Deehan, Tom Mc Mahon, Dottie Kennedy, Jim Mc Donald, Hector Naya as the basis of the team then we had new people join us Mike Rivera, Lou Romero, Paul Elhoff, Jim Byrne and Irma Crisillo and a few others. We had a man Dick Mannion, who volunteered for the mid night shift, much to the relief of the other agents. Dick had a side business where he took care of lawns. I worked with him on some days off, I had Wednesdays and Thursdays off for many years.

Dottie Kennedy could whistle like no one I ever heard. She once had a late passenger check-in and hurried him out the gate. There was a door behind the ticket counter into the baggage room and the door to the tarmac was open. Dottie watched the passenger as he ran thru the chains and he started the wrong way, she whistled a blast and everybody stopped dead, the baggage men, passengers and the man. The passenger looked back and Dottie motioned him to the correct airplane.

On the afternoon shift we (usually the first five mentioned above, the Irish mafia, plus our Cuban tenor) sometimes went for a beer after work. We would get Hector to sing for us. He had a wonderful voice and could have made it as a singer if he was ever noticed. We had many strangers, who on hearing him sing, wanted to get him on Arthur Godfrey's show. And we had Paul Elhoff who used to imitate Johnny Ray and ended up tearing his shirt off a la Johnny Ray. Paul ended up as president of TIME, a travel agent consortium that would get deals for travel agencies by nature of their volumne of collective business.

I had a bad stretch for a few months and people where considering calling me the Undertaker. The first incident happened right by our ticket counter. A man and woman had just come off 602 from Miami and were sitting on a bench outside the Brass Rail, when all of a sudden the woman keeled over and died. We sent for the doctor but he could do nothing.

The second incident was on the night shift. We had a flight running late coming from Washington, DC. It had been on time, now is was one hour late. We found that a man had a heart attack on the plane and the captain turned back to Washington to get help. We were also told that unfortunately the man died and his wife was waiting for him at our airport. It fell to me to find the wife and notify her of the death. I want to tell you that is one of the most miserable things in the World to have to do.

The third time, also on the night shift, occurred on a flight to Miami. I was notified that there was a problem on the 11:59pm plane to Miami. I ran to the gate and found the flight attendants had a man in a wheelchair at the back of the plane. I looked at him (I thought he was dead) and ran to phone for a doctor on call. The doctor (I wish I could re-member his name-I think it was Dr. Adelman) lived in Rock-away Beach. He jumped in his car and came screaming into the airport. He made it in about eight minutes. I met him and we ran to the plane. I said to him "can we get him off the plane" (I was mindful that the plane and all the passengers may have been delayed if the man died on the plane.) The doctor said yes, he grabbed the top of the wheelchair and I the bottom (I yelled back to the operations agent to get the plane out- now) and we ran to the baggage room. The doctor put him on the floor and worked like crazy to bring him back, including a six inch needle directly into the heart but was to no avail. The doctor was just great and I hope he realized how much we appreciated his work. I'm sure the man's family never knew how hard the doctor worked to try to save the man.

On the night shift there were some lulls in the action and we got to talk to many people who worked at the airport. I used to talk to the New York Times writer whose beat included the airport. We had a number of benches for the customers to sit on while waiting for the flights. The New York-New Jersey Port Authority, which ran the New York area airports, had taken quite a few benches out "for refurbishing". I was wondering to the Times man when they were going to bring them back. He told me they were not going to bring them back. He said the idea was that if the people did not have a place to sit they would walk around more and visit the concession stores in the airport and buy things. The Port Authority took about 11% of the gross as rent for the stores.

There were a couple of plane crashes while I was at Idlewild. The first was an Alitalia plane that crashed into Jamaica Bay on landing right at the end of the runway. American also crashed into Jamaica Bay on take off. There was a problem with the stabilizer breaking off. Eastern had a Connie crash on take off also. It was a foggy night about 11:30PM and as the plane went down the runway they had to cross another runway. The lights were on, on both runways and one light right at the intersection was out. The captain thought he was off the runway and tried to take off too soon. The props caught the dirt and the plane plowed in. A fire started immediately, the flight attendants got everyone off thru the fire (some were burned pretty badly). The only causality was a man who ran back into the plane to get his brief case. The flight attendant who ran the passengers thru the fire was a man named Foley and he was in the hospital with bad burns as was the female flight attendant and the first officer, who Ithink was named Green. Frank Sharpe was in charge of the problems at the hospital and had trouble with reporters trying to interview the passengers. These people were in no condition to want to talk to anyone and Frank, who was not a big man, offered to throw one the reporters down the stairs when he caught him trying to sneak in the back way. (And I believe Frank would have done it.)

We had some really nice moments at the airport also. In the Winter months we had a commuter from Palm Beach to New York. His name was Arnold Rueben (he was about 70 years old at that time) and he owned Rueben's restaurant in New York on 58th Street. He came up every Friday night and returned Sunday morning. He had a friend meet him on Fridays and bring him back on Sundays. The friend told me Mr. Rueben went directly to the restaurant and stayed there until Sunday morning, not going to bed. I found out this was where Tommy Dorsey and people like that hung out.

On Sunday mornings Mr. Rueben would come to the airport for the flight back to Palm Beach. He always flew first class and all he wanted was to get on board with his little dog and go to sleep. He had an arrangement with the captain to keep the dog in the cockpit. Every Sunday he would bring us a whole (big) cheese cake. It was the best there was. It was renown and mailed to places all over the country. I used to take a small piece over to the Brass Rail where the manager was a friend of mine, and tell him this was what real cheese cake tastes like. (The Brass Rail was always bragging about how good their cheese cake was). On days when he didn't bring a cheese cake he brought hogie like sandwiches, loaded with different meats, cheese and Russian dressing. They were excellent. I didn't realize at that time that Mr. Rueben was the man who invented the Rueben sandwich.

Mr. Rueben had given me his card and told me to go to his restaurant for dinner. I had not used it and was not really planning to do so until his friend asked me if Mr. Rueben had given me a card. I said yes but I had not used it. The friend told me Mr. Rueben had given me the card because he wanted me to use it and would be disappointed if I did not. Tom Mc Mahon had also received a card. So we went with our wives and very sheepishly handed the cards to the Maitre D'. He fell all over us and couldn't have been nicer and we had a great dinner. When I was managing the city ticket office in Miami Beach Mr. Rueben sent his grandson in to see me for some help he needed and I was happy to take care of him.

In the Spring of 1955 we had one heck of a stormy period. As usual I had Wednesdays and Thursdays off. I went to work on Friday afternoon and we had an ice storm. The traffic, airline and auto, was all screwed up. When I got off at 1:00am I had to make it home, 28 miles, on roads that were a sheet of ice. Believe it or not I was one of only 3 cars on the Southern State Parkway all the way out to Syosset.

Saturday worked out OK and then came Sunday. I went in for the afternoon shift. It started snowing about 4:00pm and kept on snowing. Finally all the roads in and out of the airport were closed. We still had a few planes come in but the passengers could not leave. I spent the night on a little green bench in the VIP room. Comfortable it was not and I didn't get much sleep. The next day was Monday and it was wild. The wind blew and the snow flew and the airport was closed. Passengers were wandering about trying to find something to eat. Fortunately I knew the manager in the Brass Rail and I got something to eat. They had locked the door because they did not have much food and very few employees.

That night Paul Elhoff and I were determined to get some sleep somewhere anything but the little green benches. About 4:00pm we found the Carey buses were running and we decided to go to the Homestead Hotel in Forest Hills for the night. We got on the bus and the driver could not even see the roadway. We were not on the road as we were going by the light poles on the wrong side. When we got to Queens Boulevard the bus driver had to stay in the middle of the road as the drifts were four feet high. He let us off in the middle of the road and we walked about three blocks to the hotel.

The next day, Tuesday, was bright and sunny. Paul and I went in early to dig our cars out of the snow, there was about two feet of snow around the cars. The afternoon shift was routine but I decided it was time to go to Miami.

I went scouting around Miami to look for a job with Eastern. I had an interview with Art Holston who was the manager of the city ticket office at 1616 Collins Avenue. He said he could use me so I came to Miami in July of 1956. Miami was still a small town in those days. I got an apartment at NE 2nd Street and 37th Street. It was a fairly nice area, that is now covered by the 112 expressway. Miami Beach was even a smaller town. There were those of us who worked there and there were some permanent residents and we all knew about each other. There were many tourists, of course, but we didn't count them as people - just tourists.

In order to work on Miami Beach we had to get a police card. We had our picture and finger prints taken, which today some would call police harassment, but we didn't mind. I believe there was some kind of unwritten rule that Black people couldn't be in Miami Beach after dark, which I found atrocious, but you did not see Black people walking around after dark. I was stopped and questioned a few times by the police when I was on the street late at night. About 11:00pm or so.

The ticket office at 1616 Collins Avenue was open seven days a week from 8:00am to 11:30pm. That meant two shifts and odd days off. Eastern had three ticket offices at that time. The 1616 office, the Columbus Hotel office on Biscayne Boulevard and the office at 71st Street and Harding Avenue, Miami Beach. Harry Dauernheim was manager at the Columbus office and Gardner Brown was manager at the 71st Street office. Shortly after I came to the 1616 Collins office Art Holston was promoted to the assistant to the District Sales manager, Ed Yarnell. Sam Privett took Arts place. Sam was a really happy go lucky guy and as was his nature was the president of the Optimist Club.

Sam stayed as the over all manager of the ticket offices for as long as I was in the ticket office and for a few years after that. He had a good friend, a Captain Whipreck(?) Who flew for Eastern and when he died he left Sam and Martha some property in North Carolina, Strawberry Ridge. Sam and Martha left Miami and Eastern and moved to around Titusville, Florida. They managed the Strawberry Ridge property. He was a nice man to work for. Sam told me Capt. Whipreck told him that he flew his plane into the eye of a hurricane on one of his trips from New York to San Juan. I don't know whether to believe him or not.

I was at 1616 Collins office for about five or six months then moved to the 71st Street office as Chief Agent. Besides Gardner Brown, the manager, we had, at various times, June Ryder, Bob Silman, Vee Lauden, Vaughn Rudokas, Fred Colton Joan Cherip, Joan Monti and others I don't remember.

There was a Delta office across the street and a Northwest

office also. National had an office two blocks away. In December of 1957 the IAM union went on strike and we closed the office for the duration. I went to work for National at their ticket office and the National agent in charge was Tom Fessler. Naturally the phone lines to the reservations office were jammed up. Here we were in the middle of the **SEASON** and the biggest airline in Miami was on strike. The office was jammed and we were trying to get thru to the res office. (No computers then). We were both hanging on to the same line waiting for an agent and talking to each other. Buddy Hackett was waiting in the office and he pipes up with "these guys got it made - they have a direct line–to each udder".

When Tom left National he was the first sales representative for Royal Caribbean Cruise Lines and they didn't even have a ship. Tom would call on agencies with a three foot ship model of the Song of Norway under his arm.

January 1st the strike ended and we all went back to work. Eastern had purchased 40 Lockeed Electras, and we had about 10 on line. It was a beautiful airplane and a very good one. It was so good it is still flying today and is also used as a hurricane hunter plane. The trouble was it was too late to be viable as a passenger plane. This was Captain Eddies biggest mistake as we spent all our money on an airplane that was obsolete. Pan Am had purchased the Boeing 707 jet and for the **57/58 SEASON** National had rented two of them from Pan Am. Everyone flying to New York wanted the jet.

Now we had to spend money we didn't have for jets. The first jet we purchased was a Boeing 720. We refused the first ones we that were allotted to us because they had water injection into the engines to boost the power. We waited for the second generation 720 which we called the 720B that did not need the water injection. This was Captain Eddies second mistake as Delta took the airplanes we refused and put them on the Miami Chicago route and took the market away from us. Most Eastern people loved Captain Eddie but he did make two big mistakes.

1960 Gardner Brown, manager of the 71 Street CTO

**Vee Louden, Joan Cherip, Fred Colton & Vaughn Rudokas
at the 71 Street City ticket office counter 1960**

In 1957 my wife and I bought a house in Pembroke Pines, which was then just a small unincorporated area. The ride to work was not too bad at the time, although there was no I-95 in those days and the traffic was not anywhere near as bad as today. But it was a long ride.

Sam Privett was manager of the office at 1616 Collins Avenue and also in charge of all the city ticket offices. Harry Dauernheim was manager of the Columbus Hotel office. In 1960 he went to the sales office as a sales representative. Sam moved over to the Columbus office and Eileen Kimball was made the manager there. Also in 1960 I was promoted to manager at the 1616 Collins Ave office. I had two assistants, Vince Turiano and Paul Gura. Later when Vince left we got Don Melloy. They were all very good men. We had Mary Benich, who was a marvel with people, Grace (Ladley) Beck who was a work horse and ate like one, although she was never over 115 pounds. Then there was Jeanine Tyre, Cookie Fisher, Bette Little, Danny Ximanes, Randy Herbst, Rita Horner, Alice Erickson, Gail Oglesby. We had as many as 24 agents in the Winter time.

In 1964 we got our the first of our 727's. It was a wonderful airplane and it became the work horse of the industry taking the place of the old DC-3. We could fly it almost anywhere in the United States. It brought jet service to a number of smaller cities.

Also in 1964 I hired the first black ticket agent in Miami. I had been at a management council meeting and talking to Bob Hach, who was the personnel manager for the Miami area. He was in charge of recruiting, testing etc of new employment candidates. He asked me if I would hire a black as a ticket agent. I said yes I would if he sent me a qualified person and not a token. A few months later he called me and said he had a lady he would send over. I asked if she was qualified and I believe he was thinking I was trying to weasel

44

out of hiring a black because he said "now you said you would hire a black don't back out now". I said no, if she is qualified I will hire her. He said she was and sent her over. She was very qualified and very sharp and I was delighted to hire her. That year I also hired a couple of other very good employees -Magda Granda and Terri Busto. Terri transferred to the airport after about a year and Magda went on to become the manager at our Little Havana ticket office and later a sales rep for Eastern, LACSA, Aero Peru and United. Magda was a very good worker and very conscientious.

The managers office, in 1960, was a good sized office. I had a large desk (complete with termites) it was face to face with the agent-secretary's desk. The agent secretary was first an agent, who worked on the counter, and secondary worked as a secretary to the manager. The first agent-secretary I had was Cookie Fisher, who if you looked into the personnel files you would not find her by that name since the personnel file had her as Marie Emanuel. She had married John Fisher who was a sales rep in Miami and later sales manager in Dallas. That did not work out but Cookie didn't change her name. Cookie later married a man named Phil Caron, who will turn up later in the book . After Cookie left to handle the convention business working at the hotels or the convention hall Jeanine Tyre became the agent secretary.

In those days men who were called transportation men or superintend of service (concierge) pretty much controlled the travel business of the tourists at their hotels. They were a good bunch of men and if they like you they would swing a lot of business your way. Bob Slaughter was the sales rep assigned to them at first and they loved him. When he died Ed Noakes was assigned to them.

Ed had been the traffic (passenger) manager at Miami Airport and was in charge of the ticket counters and the gates. After one of our strikes where most people were laid off Ed

45

was not called back. It was rumored that Frank Sharpe (vice president) did not like him and would not take him back. Ed Yarnell did like Ed Noakes and took him back as a sales rep. I think that bothered Ed Noakes for the rest of his life. Anyway Ed got along very well with the transportation men and the convention business on the Beach and they all like him.

At the ticket office we handled the transportation men by letting them by-pass the lines and crowds in the lobby of the ticket office and come directly into my office. There the agent-secretary or I took care of whatever they needed. There were a bunch of good men Dave Tolty and Bernie Coil at the Americana, Bob Metcalf at the Eden Roc, Charlie Zapp at Waldmans, Jim Byers at the Fontainebleau, Frank McCarren at the Doral, John London at the Lucerne, Jim Rudd at the Seville, Johnny Swerko at the Di Lido, Lenny Berman and George Broker at the Carillon, some I don't remember where they worked were Ted Perkins, Dave Connolly, Fred Eckelkamp, Charlie Bianca, Matty Bart and Jim Ayers. These men controlled a lot of business and were very important to us.

They were all in the Transportation Men Association. Their official titles were superintendent of service, bell captain, concierge, director of customer relations and other titles. Before the Keauffer investigation some would run Bingo games (for money) and other fund raising (for themselves) games. Most of the positions are now eliminated or redefined and their rapport with the airlines gone. Once a year Eastern held a reception for them with a fine dinner and a show. And once a year the transportation men held a party for all the association members and invited guests such as the airline people who helped them. A lot of good times were had and a lot of good friends made.

When I first got to 1616 Collins Avenue we were criticized for not selling our tour product "Happy Holidays". I started a contest with a prize for the agent who sold the most tours in a period of time. But the thing that really set the contest off was the deal I made with Bill Webber of Midway Tours. I had figured out that the agents would talk to the customers about tours and the customer took all the information and said "I'll be back". I found out the "be backs" never came back.

Getting caught in a corner during the annual VIP Party are Bob Metcalf, Ted Perkins, Dave Connolly, Fred Eckelkamp, Charlie Bianc, Matty Bart and Jim Ayers.

Midway Tours was just across the street in the DiLido Hotel stores. I asked Bill if we sold a tour could he run the tour vouchers over to the office. He said he would. So the agent wrote up the tour order, handed it to Bill and Bill gave the agent the tour vouchers. The whole deal was done in about 15 minutes, the customer was happy, the agent was happy, Bill was happy and I was happy!

Was it a success? Yes in a big way, everyone sold the tours, mostly to Puerto Rico. Vince Turiano went right off the chart I had made with 131 sales and Mary Bench was right behind.

Speaking of Bill Webber, one Winter he rented the building on the Southeast corner of Lincoln Road and Collins avenue to sell art pieces to the tourist. It was formerly a "Picken Chichen" He took me over to see the building and he showed me upstairs where they was a long narrow room with about 25 pairs of telephone wires coming out on a long counter, no telephones just the wires. It had been rumored the owner of "Picken Chicken" was a big bookie but never proven. That building is now gone and #One Lincoln Road took its place.

Another story about Bill was later when I was sales manager. I took a group of travel agents to Merida, Mexico and Bill was on the trip. There was a very nice lady on the trip from Broward county. We went to climb the temple of the magician and she was afraid to go up. Bill and I talked her into in and went up with her. She panicked when she was on top and said she did not know how she could get down is was so steep. I had noticed there was a chain down the backside of the temple so we took her over there and had her back down holding the chain, Bill on one side I on the other. That worked out fine also as Bill ended up marrying her.

We had a number of millionaires come into the office in the 60's. Mrs. Delany for one. She lived on La Gorce Island in Miami Beach. She would have her chauffeur drive her to the office in a Rolls Royce, park in front of the office and come in and sit at my desk. I would find out what she wanted, write it up and one of the agents wrote her tickets. She was a really nice lady. One day she came in for a ticket for her chauffeur to Chicago. I asked her would it be coach, she said "no first class, he likes first class." Talk about Class!

Another that came in was Harry Sley he lived on Pine Tree Drive on the water side. I think he liked Jeanine and would stand there talking to her for an hour of so. If I remember correctly his was from Philadelphia but spent the Winter in Miami Beach.

We handled another millionaire family, the Garry's, who lived on Indian Creek Island. They never came in but his secretary would come in all the time. The family owned GTE electronics.

All the airline people were friendly in those days. Bob Erickson (Alice's husband, he talked me into hiring her as an agent and that was a great choice, she was a very good agent) was manager of the United office a few doors from Eastern. He and I were good friends and both of us were tariff (fares) experts. We would discuss all the new rules and routings and figure how people were going to try and beat the airlines out of money. A lot of people around the United system called Bob for interpretation of the rules and the same for me from Eastern offices.

National Airlines ticket offices was there and Frank Payak was based there as sales manager for Miami Beach. An agent named "Chardi" was in charge of the office. Her real name was Mariana Ricchardi but few knew it. Delta had an office and the agent there was Eleanor Tyre, sister to Jeanine who worked with me. Pan Am had an office and Dave Poling worked there. He later worked as manager of inside sales for Pan Am. Northwest Airlines had a counter in the National office for a while and Toni Wilson was the agent for them. She moved to Air France as Mrs de Armis and worked there for years. We were a community to our selves.

About 1963 a man named Damaso Ayuso came into the office. He was representing the Caribe Hilton Hotel in San Juan. He talked to us about the hotel and I started thinking how would it be if I got a group of Eastern people together and took them to San Juan for three days. Could Damaso help? Yes he could and set up a REALLY GREAT price for us.

I made up a kind of brochure and sent it to the ticket offices and the reservations office. I priced the trip at $39.00 for three nights at the Caribe Hilton Hotel. This was and still is one of the finest hotels in the Caribbean. Today one dinner alone would cost you $39.00. Everyone had to get their own passes but the price included transfers between the airport and hotel, two meals a day, city tour and a trip to El Yunque, the rain forest.

The day the flight left I had to come down from Pembroke Pines (no Palmetto Expressway then) and came around the back side of the airport. I took the perimeter road, which I thought would take me right to the terminal, and ended up on Le Jeune Road going north. I was late and if I obeyed all traffic rules I would have missed the flight. Soo I made a U turn in the middle of Le Jeune Road back to the airport. You can't do that today. Fortunately you could park right in front of the terminal at that time and didn't have to find a spot in a garage. I ran through the terminal and down the concourse. As I entered the concourse I saw a very small group standing a the gate, Joan Cherip was one, and I heard her say "I think its him" I yelled its me get on the airplane. We made it, the door closed behind me and the airplane left. I was the only one who had all the information for the trip. If I missed the flight they would have been in trouble.

When we got to the hotel and I checked in the desk clerk didn't believe we had the breakfast and diners included. He brought the manager out and he read the letter I gave him from Damaso. He said OK but we could not eat in the fancy dinning room we had to eat at Al Fresco dining room off the lobby. Which worked out fine for us as among the many tables they had one big round table with a palm tree growing through it and it could accommodate all 20 of us. (See picture). That was the first trip I ran. I did another just for Eastern people and then I thought I may as well extended it to interline sales people. I used the Caribe for a few years.

BIENVENIDOS

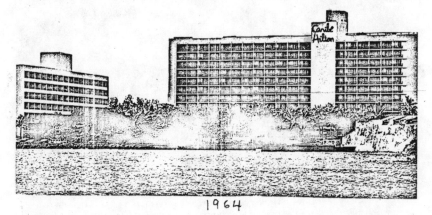

1964

A PUERTO RICO

Caribe Hilton Hotel 1964. This was our table while we were there. I can't remember all the names but across the table to the left is Diane Westrun and her husband with the flat top. To the right is Joan Cherip, Fran Brodbeck and Bruce Brodbeck.

A couple of years later I ran a trip to San Juan and we stayed at the Americana Hotel. By that time Phil Caron (Cookies husband) was the resident manager at that hotel and again we got very good rates. It was on this trip when we were sitting in the hotel lounge that Bob Hope came over to have his picture taken with us. Phil was sitting next to me and asked if I wanted to have a picture taken with Bob Hope. I said no leave him alone. But Phil said he would be glad to do it. So he jumped up got Bob over and sat him next to me for the picture. (See picture).

Eastern at that time had C-4 passes for interline people. I, not knowing any better, asked sales people from National and Delta if they wanted to go. I told them to get a letter from their pass people for Caribair Airlines to go from San Juan to St. Thomas. Well the you know what hit the fan. National had a man (Nick Boras) in charge of their pass department who (they tell me) most people at National hated. He called me and raised hell. He told me I could not invite National people, the invitation had to come from our New York office from our interline manager, Charlie Glover, to him. Then he said if he found any National people that went he would fire them. I said I was sorry I didn't know and I would tell the National people they could not go. He said no that wasn't any good and hung up. The next thing I had a call from Charlie Glover and he said any invitations like that would have to go through him. Charlie was a nice guy and everyone liked him but his idea of an interline fam trip was himself going on another airline.

I immediately called Charlie Matthews, who was the regional sales director, and told him I messed up. He said no it was all right and that if there was any problem he would run his own interline department. Well none of the National people went that time but a year later they could go. I think Nick Boras was replaced. Charlie Mathews went on to become the System Director Passenger Sales in the New

York office.

Hurricanes were a big deal in the sixties. We had three or four fairly big ones. The office had hurricane shutters that were big and heavy to cover all the plate glass windows, ten feet high. We had a company called Jones Shutters that was on call to put up the shutters when a hurricane was coming close. The first time it worked fine but the second time they never came even after numerous calls. I put the shutters up all by myself and it was all I could do, the shutters were so big and heavy. I said the next time I called and they didn't come I was not going to do it again. And I did not. The next one did come and I called and they did not come so we put up all the furniture and whatever we could and went home. When I came back the day after the hurricane there were trees down all over and garbage cans rolling in the street. As I drove past the office to park I saw water on the floor of the office and I though surely a window was gone. But no, all the water had come in under the door. No real problem.

BIENVENIDOS A PUERTO RICO

1964 Interline trip to San Juan. Picture here at Univ of Puerto Rico, Pat Carey Air Canada kneeling others can not remember their names.

Canon slide at El Moro. Tall blond is Sally Tall, Delta. Pat Carey and Bob Erickson, United.

320 N. E. First Street
Miami, Florida 33132
November 4, 1964

Mr. Sam Privett, Manager
Eastern Airlines
1616 Collins Avenue
Miami Beach, Florida

Dear Mr. Privett:

We, of National Airlines City Ticket Office, wish to thank you
and Eastern Airlines for the opportunity to visit San Juan on
your familiarization tour of October 23, 1964.

Our special thanks to Mr. Larry Green who must have put consid-
erable time and thought in planning our stay. He was the perfect
host and made the entire four days well spent and most enjoyable.

Again ... may we thank you.

Very truly yours,

National Airlines

Inez Heindle

Ruth Norris

cc: Mr. Larry Green

Larry: We enjoyed our stay in San Juan ... You were very patient
with us and we appreciate it. Thank you for your time and
trouble.

There was a night when one of the windows was broken. At 3:00am I was called by the Miami Beach police and told a window was completely broken out and they did not know if any one was in the office or if anything was taken. I had to go romping all the way from Pembroke Pines to 1616 Collins Avenue. The police told me to go in first (under my breath I said thanks a lot) and they followed me in. No one was there and nothing was taken and we figured the window just gave way from stress and heat and cold. I had to sit there until morning when I could find someone to board up the space.

While I was at the Collins Avenue office I went on the first interline fam trip that I did not organize. Varig Airlines offered a trip to Santo Domingo, in the Dominican Republic. We flew down on a Viscount, a turbo prop airplane, that Varig used to puddle jump down the islands all the way to Rio de Janeiro.

We stayed in the Intercontinental Embassador Hotel and it was a really fine hotel as it is today. It stood all alone on a big piece of high land over looking the Caribbean and it looked magnificent. Today there are high rise condos on what was open hotel land. The rooms were all furnished with French Provincial furniture. On this trip I learned a few things to do and a few not to do. Not to do was disappear as the Varig representative did, we hardly saw him at all. To do was to go to the Mason de la Cava a good restaurant set in a cave. On this trip we went way up into the mountains to a hotel called Montana. On the way up the bus broke down and we hitch hiked to the next town where we got cabs up to the hotel. We had lunch at the hotel and while we were there some rebels set fire to the forest. The firemen came to put the fire out and used the water in the hotel pool for their hose. On the way back to Santiago Domingo the escort hired the cabs to take us all the way. It was a dirt and gravel road from the hotel to the little town and had a cliff on the right side. The diver was going too fast. We asked what the markers along the road meant and he said it was where cars when off the road and people were killed. Then he floored the gas pedal and away we went We made it but as one guy in our cab from National Airlines said "I would really enjoy this if I was scared to death".

I went on a second trip while I was at this office and that was to Hawaii. Japan Airlines invited me to go. Bob Erickson of United Airlines was also invited. We had to over night in a Kennedy motel and when we woke up the next morning there was a strange glow in the room. We looked out the window and it was snowing like crazy. We got to the terminal in plenty of time but all the flights were delayed. There was a question as to if the flight would go or not or maybe even hold the fam in San Francisco which was a stop on the route to Hawaii. We finally got out at 12 or 1:00pm and it was a good trip. Got to hear Don Ho for the first time and no big crowd to buck like today. No big price either.

The trip home from New York on Eastern was a hoot. Bob and I were lucky enough to get first class. First class at that time had the famous restaurant service and it was great. Eastern had contracted with the best restaurants in New York, Chicago and Philadelphia to cater the first class section on the non stop flights to Miami and the food was excellent. When we left Hawaii Bob and I left directly from the luau to the airport. I still had on a crown of flowers from the luau when we got on the flight from New York to Miami. We kept the passengers laughing all the way home. When we left the plane the flight attendant said it was the best flight she ever had.

We had two strikes in the sixties one in 1964 lasted for over a year. The FAA had ordered the airlines to train all flight engineers (the third man in the cockpit) to train as pilots. The airlines had no choice but do as ordered. The flight Engineers

62

union objected and went on strike in a number of airlines. The office at 1616 was closed down for about three weeks. I went to work in Delta's ticket office in Fort Lauderdale. Delta was a non union airline so they continued to fly. We were re-routing passengers via Mexico City to go from Miami to Los Angeles.

When we returned and opened the office it was a mad house. (See picture) We all worked the counter. It was funny to see but the pickets even had signs in Hebrew to keep the Jewish people away. My brother-in-law was a flight engineer for TWA and their union president advised their membership not to go on strike and if they did they would probably never work for an airline again. And that is what happened. We lost a lot of good men including the afore mentioned Churchy. My brother in law stayed flying with TWA until he retired.

In 1966 Bud Schultz, system manager for travel agencies and Mr. Schackelberry? an Eastern vice president, came to see me at the 1616 Collins Avenue office. They wanted to know if I could put together a travel agents training course on fares and tariffs. At that time Eastern had a training school in the Chateau Blue in Coral Gables to teach Eastern people various subjects run by John Duffield but nothing for travel agents. I said I probably could but it would take some time to get all the materials together. They said they would give me a man to help copy the things I needed. I am sorry to say I can't remember the mans name (I think it was Earl Johnson) as he was a big help to me.

When I got the course all ready to go I taught the first two classes but told them I did not want to do that permanently so I went back to the ticket office. Unknown to us there was a aviation travel writer in one of the classes and he wrote an article on the class. I was very flattered when he wrote the three days of my session were well worth the time.

In 1967 Bud Schultz and Fred Collin decided to send me to Europe to give seminars of fares and tariffs I think as a kind of reward /training trip. Grace Ladley Beck's husband Ray Beck decided he would go with me and his company was well appreciated. They got me on Air India in first class to London and on Lufthansa in first class on the way back from Frankfurt. It was a very good trip. I gave seminars in three cities London, Paris and Frankfurt. The audience consisted of airline sales people and travel agents. We had about 40 to 50 in each session. They were very interested and the reaction was very good.

We were met in London by John Anderson, regional sales director for Europe and Ian McCrodden the sales manager for the UK. They had set up the hotel and training site plus a few meals. For Paris John Anderson went over with us. Everything over there was setup by Daniel Rebours. That worked out well also. John took us to a top restaurant called Chez Albert that was excellent. I tried to find it the next time I went to Paris but could not. I was told there were many Chez Albert's in Paris. To show you how much things have changed over the years Ray and I went to the Lido Show on the Champs Elysees. We went in for $15.00 each and told the waiter we did not like Champagne so he gave us two drinks of Scotch each and seated us right up to the edge of the stage. Today it cost $100.00 to $125.00 to go in.

The next stop was Frankfurt and we were met by Otto Hornig, the area sales manager. The session went very well and Otto when out of his way in hospitality. He set up a dinner for about 35 airline people for the German fathers day. The tradition is for the fathers to go out in the woods and drink apple wine. We stayed in the restaurant and drank apple wine. The next day he loaned us the company car to drive over to Heidelberg. I really enjoyed Germany it was not like my first visit courtesy of Uncle Sam. Ray and I got to drink some beer in the Red Ox (The Student Prince) in Heidelberg.

Flying home from Frankfurt on Lufthansa first class I tried to eat and drink everything they gave me - it couldn't be done. Just to show how it was then here is how it went. First I had a Martini, then they came around with the hors d'oeuvres. They had caviar and the flight attendant said it was real Russian caviar. I didn't know if I like caviar or not so I decided to have some and the flight attendant insisted I have a glass of vodka with it - so I did. Next was a nice white fish served with a nice white wine. After that was sauerbraten served with a good red wine and then was desert followed by champagne. To top it all off was coffee with a cordial. I was feeling pretty good by this time and had a little nap. After about 2 to 3 hours they came around with very nice sandwiches and a keg of beer. I ate the sandwich and drank the beer and then I did not feel so good. By the time we landed I made a beeline for the john. I think the beer did me in.

One of the first productions I put on was when we tied up with the Disney people when Disneyland was opened. I was able to get some costumes and all our ladies dress up for a week. We had Mary Benich, Rita Horner, Cookie Fisher, Gail Oglesby, Bette Little, Randy Herbst, Jeanine Tyre and Gracie Ladley Beck. The theme was Around the World and the costumes represented various countries. (See pictures).

BETTE LITTLE

GAIL OGLESBY

RITA HORNER

RANDEE HERBST

MARY BENICH

JEANNINE TYRE

GRACE BECK

COOKIE FISHER

68

The airline and office went through a redesign about 1964/5. A company named Lippencott & Margolis was in charge of the whole project. Anything you wanted changed was met with the phrase "that not according to L & M's design.". It took a while but I got a numbering system into the office, a la a bakery shop. They told me it didn't conform to the image and I told them we needed the system because the customers got into fights among themselves as to who was next. There is nothing like a couple of octogenarians waving their canes at each other yelling "you took my next".

<u>Training Trip to Europe 1967</u>

Ray Beck in Front of the Frankfurt Hotel

Larry Green on the Champs Elysees

First Class Meal Service on Lufthansa

Mr. F. A. Collin   New York

John S. Anderson   London

Larry Green's Visit
to Europe   May 9th 1967

Larry Green has just completed his tour of all three European
sales offices for the purpose of Visit USA and other Eastern
tariff indoctrination to local travel agency and interline
personnel.

I wish to take this opportunity of thanking you sincerely for
arranging for the visit of Larry Green as this has had a
very beneficial effect in all three European sales areas.

Mr. Green gave a most capable presentation for all concerned
and we have all received many nice compliments from those in
attendance.

I am positive now that travel agencies and interline associates
will be able to do a better job in selling Eastern as a result.

                              John S. Anderson,
                              Regional Sales Director, Europe.

JSA/gpb/V-3
c.c. Mr. W. G. Conrad
     Mr. L. Green
     Mr. O. Hornig
     Mr. I. McCrodden
     Mr. D. Rebours

I also got a window display which they were reluctant to grant. We had a large side window which everybody coming north on Collins Avenue had to see. It was a natural for an Eastern display. One more thing that the designers did not figure correctly was the new chairs for the customers. We got these beautiful low slung chairs but once the old folks were in them they couldn't get out. We had to go out in the lobby and help a number of people to get up out of the chairs.

After working for about 7 years at 1616 Collins Avenue my wife and I and 4 kids moved to Miami Beach. The commute was much better. It took Eastern about 3 months to take me out of the 1616 office and move me to downtown Miami..

Toward the end of 1967 I ask asked to go for an interview at the regional sales office. At this time Freddy Blackwell was the regional director and Art Holston was the regional sales administrator. Art Holston was leaving to work for the Eastern Travel Club.

I went in and talked to both of them and then Art took me to his office and explained the job. When he finished I asked when will I know if I got the job. Art said you already have it and to report there the first week of January.

That was the start of a great job working with a great guy, Freddy Blackwell. Fred was smart, personable, a good writer and excellent speaker. He was asked to speak at many functions. He also had a good sense of humor. He once spoke at the South By South Womens' Travel Organization meeting and they hired a streaker to run across the stage. It didn't bother Freddy at all he just stuck to the bare essentials and kept going.

The regional office was downtown Miami in the First National Bank. It consisted of Fred Blackwell, Regional Sales Director, myself as Regional Sales Administrator, Don Noonan as Regional Cargo Sales Manager, Pete Goss as Regional Group Sales Manager and Ed Williams as Regional Director of Government Affairs.

The ladies who worked with us were Mayre Burnett, who work with Fred, Jeannette Saxon who worked with Ed Williams and Carolyn Dean who worked with me. All the ladies got along well together. Jeannette Saxon, Marie Cowart who worked with Ed Yarnell and Eileen Kimball who managed the Columbus Hotel ticket office were particularly close. Marie Cowart, Jeannette Saxon and Eileen Kimball all belonged to the South by Southeast Woman Travel Organization. Marie was not just a secretary, she promoted Eastern Airlines as president of SXSE, as an official of IFWTO (International Woman's Travel Org) with branches as far away as Africa and Australia and as a member of DAMES, the district sales managers assistants.

MIAMI — Marie Cowart, secretary to Chuck Wilcoxen, was re-elected for a second term as Secretary of the International Federation of Women's Travel Clubs at it's third annual convention in Philadelphia. The organization is composed of career girls working in travel oriented industries.

MILWAUKEE — Pick a postcard . . . just one from 25,000, and come up with a winner. Tina Black did the honors while Jim Sineath, left, and Bill McCollagh of WTMJ Radio helped to spin the drum (story on page 11).

TOLEDO — Debbie McNair, Ground Hostess at Detroit Metropolitan Airport turned on her charms at the august Toledo Club, one of the few remaining bastions of male society. The Detroit Sales Office through Fred Woodward provided the decorations for this years party theme — Florida and the Caribbean. The 500 guests in attendance vied for a chance of winning the grand prize — a round trip for two from Toledo to San Juan.

PEOPLE

MIAMI — Adding their usual charm and flair to any ceremonious occasion, Lou Palacio and Larry Green, l. to r., awarded Mrs. Rosa Rodriguez the prize winning ticket for the February Interline Group Sales Contest. Employed at Alitalia, Rosa received a first class, positive space pass to any destination. The previous Interline Group Sales Contest brought in revenues in excess of $100,000.

ATLANTA — Pert Marilyn Taylor, a Bently College student at Waltham, Massachusetts wanted to go on her dream trip — but was short of funds. Wearing a sign that read "send me to the Super Bowl" she captured the imagination of a local radio station and with the help of George Tribble they arranged transportation from Boston to the Crescent City. On her return Marilyn stopped over in Atlanta for a whirlwind day of sightseeing. For Marilyn a [...]

From the Drummer March 1972, the sales communications paper. Marie Cowart just elected as an officer of the International Federation of Woman's Travel Clubs. Lou Palacio and Larry Green give an award to Rosa Rodriguez of Alitatia in our group sales contest.

The region consisted of all of Florida and Bahama Islands except the panhandle, (Pensacola). That means all the sales offices and ticket offices came under Fred Blackwell. It was a real joy to work for Fred. My job was to administer all the sales budgets and personnel in the region. The sales managers would submit their budgets to me as they saw them then I would work them over to see if they coincided with the directions from the home office. I would consolidate all the budgets and submit them to the financial people. After approval I had to make sure the sales offices stayed within the budget. Also all salary increases came thru me. One of the first things I did was to visit every ticket office in the region to see what they wanted and recommend any changes needed.

The Bahama Island Tourist Office was also in the First National Bank. The regional director was Jack Norris and he and I got to be good friends. He came to me once and said I kept telling him there was a way to take travel agents to foreign destinations without charge. And I said I know there is a way but I don't know how to do it. I called Bud Schultz in New York and he said you have to get a government order (from the foreign government). So I called Chuck Bolin in Nassau and he said he would have to ask the tourist director, Mr Chibb, for the order and he was reluctant as the last time Mr. Chibb sent an order it was turned down. I thought with Buds help it would go through smoothly. So the order was sent and the vice president of sales at the time was M. Wilson Offitt III. And he turned it down as being against IATA (International Air Transport Association) regulations.

Jack Norris came back again and said now what are we going to do. I called IATA in Montreal and asked them if there was a regulation against free fam trip tickets for travel agents. They said there was none, but there were a lot of rules that went with it. Jack asked what next and I said I would call Dick Magurno who I though was one of the smartest men in Eastern, he was a lawyer in the Washington office. I called Dick and he knew and told us how to do it. That was the start of fam trips for travel agents other than inaugural trips to new destinations or routes or new aircraft, and these were usually all free. Later I guess I started the fam trips where the agent had to pay the cost of the trip, excluding the airfare. We usually worked out a good price with the hotels and ground operators who were also anxious for new business. Jack told me quite a few times that I should be a Vice President, my trouble he said was I didn't drink with the right people.

In those days besides the government order the CAB required on international trips there would be no free time, all day time would be scheduled. Now days a government order is not needed and the airlines can do whatever they wish.

CONSEJO NACIONAL
DE TURISMO

México, D. F. Marzo 12, 1974
No. 135

Mr. K. Schultz
Manager - Agency Affairs
Eastern Airlines Inc.
Miami International Airport
Miami, Fla. 33148

Dear Mr. Schultz:

As you know, tourism is of vital importance to Mexico.

In light of this, we would be most greatful if you would assist the Mexican National Tourist Council in promoting tourism to our country.

Your assistance would come in the form of transporting 800 travel agents and travel writters on familiarization trip to Mexico during the period of six months.

We look forward to hearing from you.

Sincerely,

GUILLERMO MORENO B.
GENERAL SUB COORDINATOR

Mpt

Fred and I got along very well together he let me do my work and asked me for suggestions. I guess I had some good ideas as Fred once said to me "you make the spitballs and I'll throw them". That meant for me to come up with ideas and he would write them up to send to the home office. We did a number of things, one being the fight for Air/Sea fares which we eventually got. I had lunch with a man named Tony Massi who worked for Costa cruises. He wanted to know if we could get some special fares for cruise passengers. I told him I would try. I figured out what they should be and why we should have them and sent a memo to Freddy. Then Freddy polished up the letter and sent it to the home office.

The first one to recognize the potential for cruise passengers was Chuck Bolin who was sales manager in Fort Lauderdale. He came up with a brochure he called Zip to the Ship, which was an idea to boost cruise traffic from Port Everglades and Eastern traffic into Ft Lauderdale and boost revenue on EASTERN as the port expanded.

Chuck went on to be the sales manager for the Bahamas based in Nassau. We got to be good friends while he was there. I was over there one time and he said let get together with George Myers who was resident manager of the Nassau Beach hotel. We had a drink in George's room and made plans for dinner. However George had some chores to take care of before we left. Well one thing lead to another and we did not eat until midnight at a place called Charlie Charlies. I thought I would starve or be drunk before we got to eat.

George went on to be the general manager of the Nassau Beach Hotel and could he throw a party. The Bahamas Tourist board and the Nassau Paradise Island Promotion board decided to have one big fam trip for travel agents from all over the US. There were about 1000 attendees, the biggest fam I ever heard about. It was about 30 years ago and I still remember it well. George turned the top floor (7th) of the Nassau Beach Hotel into a party. He had four different kinds of bars set up and a band playing in one of the rooms. I left at 3:00am but was told the party went on until breakfast. The final dinner was set in the Lowes Paradise Island hotel grand ballroom which could accommodate all 1000 agents plus a number of local dignitaries. The evening started with an open liquor bar for the first hour. The tables were set with balloons, favors and noise makers such as cow bells. The dinner was excellent and the wine flowed. Then they brought the Gumbay dancers in and everyone was up dancing. A fitting end to very successful promotion and display of hotels and attractions. George went on after a few years to be Vice President and General Manager of Resorts International, which today is Atlantis. And George now operates the Cable Beach resort, a really fine hotel.

Another idea was to get an interline program going in Southeast Region. There was a lot of business out there that we were not getting. I organized a regional interline committee with a sales rep from each city. We had Dave Moore from Miami, Clint Franke from Jacksonville, Bob Carr from Tampa, Terri Tafey from Orlando and I don't remember the others. John Siefert was now the system interline sales manager and he was very much in favor of taking other airline sales people on EASTERN to show our good service, our destinations and to create good will toward EASTERN. I had a sales person from another airline tell me after we started this program that up to then most other airlines considered EASTERN stuck up, unfriendly and that we didn't need any help from outside.

Mr. F. L. Blackwell, Jr.   MIASO

L. C. Green   MIASP

Air Sea Fares   December 4, 1972

We are in need of year round Air-Sea GIT fares from our Northern and
Western cities into Miami/Fort Lauderdale area.

Miami is now the cruise capital of the World. The cruise company
salesmen are out in the Northern and Western states selling their
product from Miami and they have been very successful. Their success
has caused the cruise lines to look for a means to transport their
customers to Miami. Royal Caribbean has partially solved this by
chartering World Airways from California every week. Costa Lines
is chartering TIA from New York and McClough Airlines from Chicago
and Cleveland.

Most cruise lines prefer to do business with scheduled airlines if
they can get a fare attractive enough for their clients. The fare
then should be:

1. Saturdays only.

2. Minimum of 7 days.

3. Maximum of 21 days.

4. Travel together on going portion only, permission to return
   individually.

5. Year round with blackout dates at Christmas, New Years and
   Easter.

6. Lower than family plan for two people.

7. Possible two levels of fare for off peak and high season. The
   off peak to be at least as cheap as the minimum.excursion fare.

3. Minimum in group, 15 to 20 peaople.

9. Non-affinity.

There is also the possibility of providing a fare on Fridays and Mondays
for the three and four days cruises to Nassau.

These GIT fares will not be diversionary according to surveys made
by Costa Lines. Their surveys show 85% of the people on their charters
would not have flown except as a means to go on the cruise.

Attached is a list of the ships leaving from Miami and their capacity.

80

SHIP	CABINS	MIN. PASSENGERS	PORT	FREQUENCY
Frederico "C"	402	804	Pt. Everglades	Every Saturday
Angela Lauro	400	800	" "	Every other Saturday
Flavia	377	754	Miami	Friday and Monday
Song of Norway	377	754	"	Every Saturday
Nordic Prince	374	748	"	Every other Saturday
Sun Viking	332	764	"	Every other Saturday
Starward	277	554	"	Every Saturday
Skyward	363	726	"	Every Saturday
Southward	366	772	"	Every other Saturday
New Bahama Star	250	500	"	Friday and Monday
Emerald Seas	400	800	"	Friday and Monday
Boeheme	225	450	"	Every Saturday
Mardi Gras	438	876	"	Every Saturday

Mr. A. Robert Simpson   MIAKP

F. L. Blackwell, Jr.   MIASO

Air Sea Fares on the High Seas   December 13, 1972

Bob, here is another voice from the high seas, looking to
establish those kind of rates that will make an alliance
with Eastern beneficial to both the Costa Lines and to our
favorite airline.

Since you are examining the whole broad scope leading to an
analysis of further associations with a variety of cruise lines
and embracing consideration of a variety of prospective air sea
fares, I am wondering if you could give the attached document
from Miami Group Sales Manager, Larry Green, a reading and let
us have your thoughts on the best way to proceed.

I know from conversations with Larry that these people are most
anxious to get with us for a full exploration of further ideas
and if you feel that would be in order, let's pick a time and
date and do just that.

                        ORIGINAL SIGNED BY
                    FREDERICK L. BLACKWELL, JR.

                            F. L. Blackwell, Jr.

FLB/dbk
Attachment

cc: C. Small - MIASO
    L. Green - MIASP   THIS COPY FOR

                                82

Mr. F. L. Blackwell, Jr.   MIASO

A. R. Simpson   MIAKP

FLORIDA AIR/SEA FARES   January 9, 1973

Fred, as we discussed yesterday we are pushing for both individual
and group rates for air/sea applicability via Florida points. At
this stage I would estimate something like an ITX fare for the individual and some group rate slightly lower. As you know, we would
like to do a joint program with Norwegian Caribbean as a starter
rather than Costa Lines. This stems primarily from some bad ex-
periences we have had in the past with Costa and their insistence
on continuing to use supplemental carriers in our major markets.
I have passed on Larry Green's suggestions re conditions to Bill
Masters for his consideration in developing the filing. If approved,
I would anticipate a start up date of late spring or early summer
on a year round program.

                          ORIGINAL SIGNED BY
                          A. R. SIMPSON

                             A. R. Simpson

ARS:dl

cc: Messrs. L. C. Green
              W. D. Masters (attachment)

                                83

John Siefert set up our first fam trip (May 24, 1968) and paid for the hotel and tours. The trip was to Mexico City using our route via New Orleans. We stayed at the Alfer Hotel and they treated us wonderfully. They even threw a tequila cocktail party for us and had a Mariachi band to play for us. It was my first visit to Mexico City as it was with most participants on the trip. We saw many of the famous places in and around Mexico City, the Zocalo, the Cathedral, the presidential palace, with the Diego Rivera murals, the archeological museum, the archeological zone at Teotihuacan, and the Del Lago restaurant in Chapultepec Park. I did not see the Ballet Folklorico as I was not aware of what it was. I did see it the next time and every time after that. The trip was a rousing success and we had sales managers to ticket agents on the trip. (See list). John and Mac McLaughlin (interline manager later) helped me with C-4 passes with the service charge waived for numerous trips.

The first full year of the committee was very successful as shown by Fred Blackwell memo to George Lyall, vice president of sales. We achieved 104.2% of our goal and increased revenue in 1969 to 27.3% over 1968.

interoffice correspondence

 EASTERN

TO:	Mr. G. A. Lyall	**ADDRESS:**	New York
FROM:	F. L. Blackwell, Jr.	**ADDRESS:**	Miami
SUBJECT:	Southeast Regional Recap - 1969	**DATE:**	March 12, 1970

On Sunday last, March 8, 1970, we gave out the last golf trophy that we in the Southeast Region will be responsible for on behalf of Eastern Airlines this year. Therefore, as we return to our real world, we want to take a moment to sound a trumpet toot or two in behalf of the 1969 happenings in the Southeast Region.

Absenting a regional merchandising manager to prepare colorful, dramatic, promissory documents for us, we adopted a course of action which could only be labeled, "By your deeds, ye shall know them". Therefore, let me help you to 'know' the people of the Southeast Region - 1969 variety:

1. The Eastern Airlines system increase in passenger boardings 1969 was 4.1%. In the Southeast Region, it was 9.6%.

2. The corporate increase in revenue was 17%. The Southeast Regional increase in revenue year over year was 22.6%.

I think it is safe to say in both instances the contribution of the Southeast Region added materially to the corporate increase figures, and that, therefore, it may be assumed that the real disparity was considerably greater.

Turning next to the final 1969 CSR runs, we note that in the seven measurable categories of revenue sales sources, the Southeast Region, and the Southeast Region alone exceeded assigned goals in every single one of these sources.

Results suggest reasons...the following is an evaluation of the 'how' and 'why' of our 1969 revenue source accomplishments:

1. EASTERN OUTLETS - achievement in this area was 100.9% of quota, up an actual 23% over 1968.

   We had the very able help of Reservations and Customer Services personnel. This activity truly represented a team effort.

    a. Reservations increased their Speed Mail ticket
        distribution dramatically this year.

    b. Our friends at the field ticket offices handled
        the heavy burden of last minute tickets with real
        dispatch.

    c. Our own ticket office managers and supervisors
        spent any 'slow' time they had available in making
        person-to-person calls on neighboring businesses
        and travel agents.

2. TRAVEL AGENTS - achievement in this area was 100.5% of
    quota, representing a 20.7% increase over 1968.

    The following were critical aids in this accomplishment:

    a. Window displays.

    b. Newsletters.

    c. Travel agency advisory conferences.

    d. Marketing training school courses.

    e. Familiarization trips (which we were able to have
        allocated to the Southeast Region for the very
        first time).

    f. "Thanks For The Business" cocktail parties and dinners.

3. VOLUME TICKETING - here we reached 112.9% of our quota which
    represented almost a 50% increase over 1968.

    We really zeroed-in on this category in 1969, scoring heavily.
    We used every bit of material available to us and blended in
    a few gimmicks of our own:

    a. We expanded our teleticketing accounts.

    b. We used CSA as it is supposed to be used - i.e., to
        identify accounts and to become personally familiar with
        large volume users on a first-name basis.

    c. We capitalized on our Women-In-Travel program embellished
        by local luncheons of our own.

    d. We organized special merchandising parties and get-togethers
        for the fashion trade and for the department stores under
        expert guidance of our Miami district sales manager, and
        his fashion gal, Miss Flo Alexander.

4. INTERLINE - here is a biggy...we reached 104.2% of
    our quota in this vital area, up 27.3% over 1968.

    Our calatyst here was our own Interline Committee
    formed within the Southeast Region, comprised of
    representatives of each and every district, and chaired
    by Regional Sales Administrator Larry Green. This group
    was charged with the responsibility of concentrating
    on interline revenue. Through this medium, one sales
    representative in each district busied himself developing
    internal programs within his district, aimed at grabbing
    an increasing share of the incremental revenue potential
    that is inherent in interline business.

    Regionally, we oversaw and directed the following campaign
    ingredients:

    a. Interline give-a-ways.

    b. "Coffee and" get-togethers and slide presentations
        at interline airport installations and other airline
        reservations sales offices.

    c. Our new C-4 program which worked wonders.

    d. We conducted 'product knowledge' tours with our
        interline associates.

    3. Our own familiarization trips to the Bahamas and
        St. Croix scored very, very favorably.

    With regard to the all important bottom-line figure, that of
total revenue, we can report to you that every one of our districts
was able to share in our over-quota performance:

                    Fort Lauderdale. 107.3%
                    West Palm Beach. 104.3%
                    Nassau 102.1%
                    Orlando 101.0%
                    Miami 100.9%
                    Tampa 100.7%
                    Jacksonville 100.1%

    Sales activity and resultant revenue achievements, as a result
of that activity, are perhaps the most meaningful statistics of all,
but they were not accomplished without concern for proper cost control.

We in the Southeast Region were able to end 1969 with surpluses
of $9,501.00 in our Field Sales (370) budget, and $25,151.00 in
our City Ticket Office (340) budget.

So much for 1969.

1970 is already well under way. We can spot as readily as anyone
else the recessional clouds already appearing on our radar scope,
but we see them simply as new challenges...far more troublesome
perhaps than those we met in 1969, but we licked those and we are
confident of our ability to overcome any obstacles that 1970 may
have in store for us. That confidence is buoyed both by the
increasing attention being given the Southeast Region through the reorganization of our Planning and Advertising Department, and what
we are sure will be the local benefits of your recently revitalized
Field Sales staff support setup.

We said at the outset of this brief paper that it was intended to
be an unmuted blast of one region's trumpet, but I am just so
doggone proud of the Southeast Field Sales gang that I couldn't
resist it.

                                    F. L. Blackwell, Jr.

At that time our district sales managers were Ed Yarnell in Miami, Henry Johnson in Ft Lauderdale, Tom Sherwood in Palm Beach, Bob Winn in Orlando, John Ingle in Jacksonville, Wayne Bevis in Tampa. Chuck Bolin in Nassau. Bob Hanson worked in Orlando for Bob Winn but looked after Daytona Beach. Jim Frizell was our sales representative in Freeport. Most of the other cities we flew into were covered by the closest sale office. Ed Northcutt was district director of Public Affairs in Tallahassee but kind of looked out for sales also.

Whenever Fred would go away on vacation or other business he would leave me in charge of the region. I think I earned the respect of all the sales managers as I did my best to help them when ever I could. When the Region broke up Bob Winn told me that I had been real helpful to him and if he was ever in position to help me he would do so.

They didn't know it but I handled all their pay raises when ever they came. I would ask Fred to rate the managers as "A" "B" "C" or "D". From there I worked out how much each man got. Each position had a grade assigned to it, all sales managers were not the same grade. Depending on the size and importance of the city, the larger the city the higher the grade. I also gave them guide lines for the sales reps increases.

May 24, 1968

WELCOME ABOARD EASTERN AIRLINES

It is our pleasure to welcome you on this weekend tour to Mexico City and to have the opportunity of acquainting you with our service to this exciting country.

As the sales force of the industry, you have directed many customers over our routes and we are truly appreciative of your support.

We feel that this familiarization trip will assist you in recommending and selling Eastern to your customers and to assure you of our continued excellence in service.

My sincere thanks for joining us, and best wishes for a most enjoyable weekend.

Cordially,

John M. Siefert
Manager
Interline Sales

<u>INTERLINE FAMILIARIZATION TOUR</u>

MEXICO CITY

May 24 - 26, 1968

Larry Green - Eastern Airlines - Tour Conductor

Maureen Healy - National
Geneva Morefield - National
Donna Burger - Northwest
Ronnie Makar - Northwest
Dottie Smith - National
Carol Fuller - Delta
Olga Greenop - TWA
Virginia Holsapple - SAS
Lorie Konis - Lufthansa
Norma Kinsella - Eastern

Ernie Bell - National
Sam Hill - National
Ernest Elder - BOAC
Jose Martinez - Alitalia
Bill Cotton - Delta
Jack Mobley - Delta
Jack Weir - Delta
Ed Woodell - United
Jim Parker - TWA
Bob Sign - Northeast
Carl Garrell - United

Larry Green &
Bob Sign (NE)
in front of the
Pyramid of the
Sun
Can't remember
the ladies

Ivan Paganatsi (NE)
the lady?
Larry Green
climbing the
Ptramid

In 1968 we had a Regional Sales Administrators meeting in Bermuda, the first time I was ever there. Walt Rodgers was our host as he was the top man for Eastern in Bermuda. I had known Walt from when he was Reservations manager for Eastern in Miami. It was there I learned that a family can have only one car, plus they could have motor bikes. On one day we all rented motor bike and inspected the Island. A very neat and beautiful place but very small. I met all the regional administrators one who was John DeRose who went on to work in the home office, the Miami office on special projects and founded the Miami Retirees Association.

One day I walked into Fred's office and he was very white and upset. I asked him what was the matter and he said "Wally Conrad, vice president of sales, wants me to fire Ed Yarnell". Now Freddy liked Ed very much, as did I, and Ed had given Freddy his first break at Eastern. This was a question of the top man not knowing the strengths of his managers. Ed was a good solid business man. Someone you could count on. I don't know anyone who knew him that did not like him or respect him.

Fred delayed the decision as long as possible. Henry Johnson in Ft Lauderdale had died leaving the job open up there. So the Fort Lauderdale sales managers job was open. He called Conrad and told him he wanted to put Ed Yarnell in that position. I was sitting there as Fred augured with Conrad. Finally Fred said "you told me I could put in anyone I wanted and I want Ed Yarnell." Finally Conrad gave in. Ed stayed in that job until Ed Williams, Regional Director of Government Affairs retired and Ed took that job until he retired. It would have been a shame to lose a good man like Ed Yarnell on some VPs whim.

Norm Koppen was moved in as the district sales manager. Norm had been in our cargo department and also had sales experience at American Airlines. He stayed at that position until the big shake up and was moved back to cargo. He left after a few years and started his own travel agency called Viking Travel. He did well.

In 1967 or 68 Eastern wanted the route from Miami to the Virgin Islands. Pan Am held the route but never flew it because they didn't know how to do it with the very short runway on St Thomas. Eastern asked the FAA for permission to demonstrate how it could be done. At that time the only way to get there was to fly to San Juan and then take Caribair DC-3 to St Thomas.

Eastern took a 727 down for the demonstration and the whole populace in St Thomas and then St Croix came out to see the jet land. The trick was to arrive in St Thomas with a low amount of fuel, off load passengers to St Thomas, pick up passengers for Miami, fly to St Croix, off load passengers for St Croix, fuel up to max, load passengers to Miami and fly home. St Croix had a long runway and it was no problem to carry a full load. Pan Am said thanks very much and started flying the route. Eastern, however, got the route also not much after that.

Bill O'Connor, Larry Green, Jack Flaugh and John DeRose

We all rented motor bikes to see the islands. Jack Flaugh, John Cox,
Sandy Donehoo, Harry Battaile, Larry Green, John DeRose,
Bill O'Connor and Rolfe Andersen

95

I had the opportunity to be on radio talk shows a number of times. Ethel Blum had a travel show on Saturday mornings and I was her guest on three different occasions. Below is a clipping from the radio highlights around 1980. The clipping has Louise Harrigan who is really Ludwig Harrigan. He was a Virgin Islander and the Southern States director for the Virgin Islands Tourist Board. We were on for two hours and then the station had a problem with the following show and we stayed on for the third hour. It is easy to talk about some place you really like and believe in. I was also on a local TV show one time with Ernie Lara of Travelwise.

Speaking of the Virgin Islands and Caribair the only time I thought I was not going to make it was on a flight from St. Thomas to San Juan on a Caribair DC-9. Most airlines had 95 seats on the small DC-9 but Caribair had 128 seats. Well, the flight was full and the Captain taxied to the hill at the end of the runway, stood on the brakes and revved up the engins. Down the runway we went but not lifting at all. I was sitting in the aisle seat on three seat side and a lady who was on the fam leaned over the man next to me and said "Larry I don't think..." I interrupted her and said "leave me alone I don't want to think about it". When we got to the end of the runway (which ended at the water) I believe the Captain just retracted the wheels and we went flat out over the water. I kept thinking "we're going to get wet, we're going to get wet". Thank God the airplane finally nosed up and we were all right.

About 1969 the all the sales people in Miami decided to start a sales organization which they called MAARS, Miami Airline Sales Representatives. Vic Leonard of Air Canada and Bob Neiman of Air Jamaica were the main movers. We used to meet for breakfast at 8:00am at the Everglades or the Columbus Hotel. I took the group on their first fam trip to St Croix. We stayed at the Estate Carlton which was great. We had nine jeeps and I was leading the caravan as I was the only one who knew where we were going and how to get there. I had to make sure all the people I had driving knew to stay on the left side of the road. I saw the turn off for the hotel as I went passed and had to turn around. The turn around was something as else I turned into a curved driveway of a private home and all eight jeeps followed me. I often wonder what the residents thought was happening to them. (A police raid?)

MR. J. I. BARRAQUE	AERONAVES DE MEXICO
MR. LEONARD BRIDGES	ICELANDIC AIRLINES
MR. RALPH CARR	SCANDINAVIAN AIRLINES
MR. DAVID CONOVER	NORTHEAST AIRLINES
MR. W. E. COTTON	DELTA AIRLINES
MISS MARTHA DRAGON	ALASKA AIRLINES
MR. JOHN DUFF	JAPAN AIR LINES
MR. S. E. GOOD	SCANDINAVIAN AIRLINES
MR. KENNETH GREIG	UNITED AIR LINES
MR. JOHN HEDENGREN	BRITISH OVERSEAS AIRWAYS
MR. ROGER HEMBROUGH	BRANIFF INTERNATIONAL
MRS. MARCIE HUGHES	VARIG AIRLINES
MR. WILLIAM KELLY	UNITED AIR LINES
MR, ROBERT LAWSON	LUFTHANSA AIRLINES
MR. VIC LEONARD	AIR CANADA
MR. JOSE MARTINEZ	ALITALIA AIRLINES
MR. A. MARTINEZ-FONTS	BRITISH WEST INDIAN AIRWAYS
MR. FRANK MASDEU	AIR JAMAICA
MRS. NANCY McLEMORE	TRANS WORLD AIRLINES
MR. FRANK MENICK	ICELANDIC AIRLINES
MR. ROBERT NEIMAN	AIR JAMAICA
MRS. JAYNA PAYAK	DELTA AIR LINES
MR. FRANK PAYAK	NATIONAL AIRLINES
MR. DAVID POLING	PAN AMERICAN AIRWAYS
MR. MICHAEL SEXTON	IRISH INTERNATIONAL AIRLINES
MR. ROBERT SIMONI	ALITALIA AIRLINES
MR. ROBERT SOPHER	BRANIFF INTERNATIONAL
MR. RUDY URRUELA	BAHAMAS AIRWAYS
MR. RICHARD VEHRING	UNITED AIR LINES
MR. ELON WEST	NORTHEAST AIRLINES

MR. & MRS NORM KOPPEN	EASTERN AIRLINES
MR. LARRY GREEN	EASTERN AIRLINES

◄◄Snorkeling over the underwater trail

Our first mate in the yellow bikini➤➤
Lou Greenwell behind

◄◄Swimming off shore Buck Island

One of the highlights of the trip was the underwater park at Buck Island. Frank Payak and I had never been snorkeling before and we were struggling to keep up with our swimming guide who was a 23 year old girl who could swim like a fish.

We had about 23 airlines represented on the trip.(see list).

I was elected president of MAARS for the year 1973/74 taking over from Dave Poling of Pan Am. The installation was at the Sonesta Beach Hotel on Key Biscayne. (See picture)

Seeing as the Bahamas was part of our region I got to know many people in the Nassau and Freeport. Nassau was a fairly stable town while Freeport was growing and building many homes for expatriates who wanted to live in the sun. We had stateside Eastern people in both communities. The administration of the sales people fell to me. We had to pay the Bahama Government $500.00 a year per each employee for work permits. Today the work permit is $5000.00 a year, if you can get one. For the stateside people working over there I had a formula to work out their pay. It included a % bonus for working away from home and a cost of living increase based on the cost of living in the Bahamas.

We had one employee, Bill Reynolds, who managed the Freeport ticket office. Bill got into an argument with an immigrations inspector on the way in to Freeport about his needing a passport. I got the call the next day to "take him off the island". I use this to today as my example in my advise "never quarrel with a customs or immigrations inspector." I had to replace him immediately and I asked Gardner Brown in the 71st Street CTO if he would like the job. He accepted and I thought I was doing him a favor. I was not. Bill Reynolds took over Gardner's job.

Besides Chuck Bolin in Nassau we had Bill Biermann, station

manager, Charles Scully, airport supervisor, Joe Martin was reservation manager and Hank Jara was ticket office manager. Charles Scully was our station manager in London when Eastern flew there. He helped me in London when I had a group of travel agents on a fam trip on another airline (non competitive) and they had schedule problems. The airline flew us to London then had us booked on Pan Am to New York. There we would have to overnight and catch an Eastern flight to Miami the next day. Charley gave us space on Eastern, which was the first agent's group on Eastern's London flight. We had to overnight in London but the Eastern flight went non stop to Miami.

Joe Martin relates the story of when he first got to Nassau and no one knew him (he thought). The casinos in Nassau were for visitors only. Local people and people who worked in the Bahamas where not allowed to gamble. Joe went into the casino to gamble and was picked up by two men who took him to the managers office. The manager insisted Joe worked in Nassau and Joe said no. They kept after him until Joe finally admitted he was going to work there. He still carried the canceled check for $250.00 around with him to remind himself not to gamble.

2007/09/20

Dave Poling of Pan Am turns the presidents gavel of the Miami Association of
Airline Sales Representatives over to Larry Green of Eastern Airlines at the
installation dinner July 14, 1973 at the Sonesta Beach Hotel, Key Biscayne.

Freeport had a number of characters, Jim Frizell was our sales man over there and Preston Locke was an executive with the promotion board. Every time I went over there they had parties in someone house. A couple of real nuts who had a good time while it lasted but those things never do. The Bahamas government cracked down on the number of non Bahamians working in the islands. Jim was sent to Washington and Preston surfaced as general manager of the Green Turtle Lodge on Green Turtle Key. On a trip one time to Treasure Key Preston came over by motor boat to pick up Jim Connell, of the Miami Herald, and myself to have lunch and see the Lodge. It was a beautiful place and still is and very laid back

Eastern had established a training center at the Chateau Blue motel in Coral Gables. FL with John Duffield as the director. The school would bring in various Eastern people to teach them new procedures. One year they brought in all the sales managers, half at a time. We had some really fine men who were the soul of Eastern and who looked after the image and reputation of Eastern Airlines. Here is a picture taken at the end of one of the sessions with half of the sales managers. (See picture)

Then in the middle of 1970 the company decided to reorganize the whole company. EASTERN brought in a management consultant company to do the reorganization. In my opinion it was a disaster. Braniff Airlines did the same thing hiring a different management consultant company. It seems strange that EASTERN had an organization with a vice president of sales and a sales force reporting to him, while Braniff had a city manager type organization where the airport manager was also in charge of sales. Our consultant recommended Eastern to have a city manager type and the Braniff consultant recommended they go to a separate sales force. I guess if you are being paid $100,000.00 or more to consult you can't say every thing is fine keep it as is. It cost

EASTERN and it took five or six years to get it back to a separate sales force. Miami and New York did not go under the station manager position but reported direct to the division vice president.

The job of running an airport for a large airline is a big enough job for anyone without taking on the sales responsibility. One or the other interests has to suffer and it did.

Anyway that broke up the sales team and moved everyone around. Fred was moved to the home office, Don Noonan was moved to the cargo facility as manager. Pete Goss wanted the sales managers job in Ft Lauderdale and he figured Ed Yarnell would be moved to city manager/station manager. Instead the powers that be made him the city manager/station manager and left Ed as sales manager. And I was left looking for a job. Bill Lindsay, who had been the system Manager Field Sales Administration & Controls, told me that I was the best administrator that he had. However all the other administrators seem to get jobs right away and I was left looking. A very low point in my life at Eastern.

SALES MANAGERS SEMINAR, CHATEAU BLUE, CORAL GABLES APRIL 1969

Top row: J. McCrodden- LON, R. Mulford- BOS, J. Fisher- DAL, A. Lally- PVD, F. Knox-SAT, C. Lewis-DTT, Robinson-MKE, K.Sheldon- CLE, R. Rehm-CVG, F. Tankersley-MSP, L. Beasley-HOU, K. Fraser-NYC
Bottom row: J. Webb-PDX, H. Gobeil-BHM, H. Cruz-LAT, E. Byrd-PHL, J. Dawson-YUL, J. Dishong-CLT, J Ingle-JAX, L. Green-ML

105

Dick Bergner came in as regional vice president of sales and service for south Florida and the Bahamas. Chuck Wilcoxen was sales manager reporting directly to Bergner. As I said New York and Miami sales reported directly to the Vice President and all the other sales managers reported to the city manager called the district manager sales and service. This manager was based at the airport and the real job was running the airport and sales was secondary. (Some will argue this).

Dick Bergner offered me the job of Manager of departure services at the airport but I had worked the airports of eight years and did not want to go backwards. Finally they gave me the job of Regional Manager of Group and convention Sales based in the Miami sales office. The sales office was in the Pan American Bank building and the regional office had been in the First National Bank building. All though the space in the First National Bank was smaller Wilcoxen wanted to move the sales office into the vacated regional office, which had more prestige, and he did. He had the old regional sales Directors office and I had my old office back. Bob Hayden, who was supervisor of sales and a really good man, had Don Noonans old office, Hector Cruz, who was Manager of Latin American Sales had Pete's old office, Jim Epting and Harry Dauernheim had an office and the rest of the sales force was squeezed into one room. It was really crowded. Marie Cowart came over as Wilcoxen's secretary along with Nedra Swasey and Cathy Hasselbach, Ana Duarte, who was Hector Cruz's secretary also came over. I believe she had to sit in the hallway.

Soon after Jim Epting and Harry Dauernheim retired and Ed Noakes, Chuck Stinnett and Lou Greenwell moved into their office. Everyone was crowded into the back room and I felt I should help out so I invited Luis Palacio to move his desk in with me. We got along like two brothers.
I had been trying to get someone assigned to interline sales

(without other duties) in Miami for five years. (See memo written in 1966). Finally Chuck Wilcoxen made Luis the interline man and that was an excellent choice as Luis very gregarious, had a good personality and could speak to the Latin American airlines in their own tongue. We received a lot of business from these people until we started flying in to South America. Luis also did a great job with the trans Atlantic airlines as most did not fly into Miami at that time, we got a lot of business from them also.

Bob Hayden did a very good job of supervising all the sales representatives and had another talent, that of writing parodies of songs to fit whatever production we did. Some where quite funny. Bob had the distinction of being hijacked to Cuba when he was on a plane coming from New York. They were taken to Veradero Beach for over night on a bus. While on the bus the Cuban escort found out Bob worked for Eastern and asked if he knew Hector Cruz. Small World. Bob was also involved in the airlift to bring Cuban children into the United States and get them to safe places. It was all very secret and Bob got no credit for all the work he did including getting up in the middle of the night to go running to the airport.

Mr. C. F. Yarnell   MIASO

L. C. Green   MIACApl

INTERLINE   6-23-66

Fact 1.   We compete with every airline from Miami.

Fact 2.   We are the only airline which does compete with all airlines and in many cases we are the only competition.

Fact 3.   There is no reason for any other airline's employees to love us since we are their competition - and a tough one at that.

Fact 4.   Other airlines are compatible - such as Northwest can refer New York passengers to National and National can refer Chicago passengers to Northwest.

Fact 5.   Our interline figures are a farce. Accounting assigns to interline revenue all revenue taken in on other airline tickets. Millions of these dollars are actually brought into the company by the city ticket offices and the field ticket offices.

Locally here in Miami we should be doing much more to obtain interline business. About the only way we have to increase business is by prevailing on personal relationships. Unfortunately, many people gage their relations by what you have done for them or what you can do for them.

I strongly urge two plans of action to increase this business.

1.   Provide our interline man with some give aways such as pens with our name and interline number, telephone dialers and a fancy card with a dime for a coffee break.

2.   Set up some interline trips on Eastern for sales personnel. These trips do not cost Eastern any money out of pocket and are the best way to realize new business for the following reasons.

    a.   We let the interline people actually experience our excellent service and equipment.

    b.   We familiarize them with one of our destinations.

    c.   The last and most important reason is that these people feel obligated to us. They feel they owe us something for the nice trip and they come back eager to sell something on Eastern to repay us.

                                                L. C. Green

LCG:jt

cc: Mr. S. S. Privett

Hector Cruz was of course in our office. He was in charge of South American sales. He had a sales rep work for him and they would travel all over South America asking for business for Eastern. He was a very cordial and gentlemanly person who I think everyone liked. He was a good friend. Hector had Jorge Diaz Silvera and then Max Martinez to work with him, The sales office was lucky to get Max when that job was phased out. When Eastern took over Braniff's South American routes Hector was moved into the Home Office, which he really did not like.

Toward the end of 1971 Chuck Wilcoxen was made Sales Manager in New York and Don Noonan moved in as Sales Manager for Miami. Dick Bergner was still Vice President for South Florida and the Bahamas.

It was my job to organize any kind of group that moved. I had a travel agent group I was taking to Puerto Rico for the opening of the Cerromar Hotel. Eastern owned the Dorado Beach Hotel and the Cerromar was built on the same property about a half a mile away. The two hotels were run by Rockresorts. They ran some very elite hotels such as the Dorado Beach, Canel Bay on St Johns, Little Dix Bay on Virgin Gorda and the Monakea Hotel in Hawaii. These hotels were unique and in high demand from corporation presidents, CEOs and other rich people. The Cerromar was a fine hotel but not in league with the others and Rockresorts did not know how to operate it. Eastern ended up turning the two hotels back to the mortgage company. Hyatt Hotels now runs the properties and they do very well.

At one time I had a group of 80 golfers who wanted to use the Cerromar and I worked out all the details except one. The group wanted the golf carts for free. As much as I tried I could not get the management to give the carts. They lost the group to the hotel and Eastern lost the group to Puerto Rico.

Anyway Dick Bergner decided to accompany the group. I tried to get him a suite but the hotel would not do it. I don't think Bergner ever forgave me for that. A few years later Bill Gregg took over as Vice President for South Florida and the Bahamas and he was the beneficiary of that incident.

Eastern started the Miami- Jamaica route in July 1975. It was decided to take some city officials and some corporate accounts to Jamaica. I was in charge of setting up the arrangements. At the same time Intercontinental Hotels was opening up their Rose Hall resort (now the Wyndham Rose Hall). Pete Southerland was President of Intercontinental Hotels and he was invited to come as we were using his hotel. I made sure Bill Gregg got the biggest suite in the hotel. It was a good trip, we showed them around the Montego Bay area and we took them rafting down the Martha Brea River. The final dinner was a grand affair. I got a few nice letters from a couple of city officals. I had one from Steve Clark, the mayor but lost it.

The group and charter business was not an easy task. I had to dig around to find business and I had to be careful not to step on anyone's toes. The whole country was someone's territory. I got to meet a lot of people and I took whatever business I could get.

City of Miami, Florida

VICE MAYOR
J. L. PLUMMER, JR.
CITY HALL

August 15, 1975

Mr. Larry Green
Sales Executive
Eastern Airlines
#700 First National Bank Bldg.
100 South Biscayne Blvd.
Miami, Florida 33131

Dear Larry:

I would like to take this opportunity to express
to you and to the other personnel at Eastern
Airlines my appreciation for all of the effort
that made our recent trip to Montego Bay, Jamaica
the success that it was. It surely was a most
enjoyable and a most memorable visit.

The service aboard the flight, as well as the
hotel accommodations and the planned activities,
was excellant. Once again, the people at Eastern outdid themselves!

Sending my sincere best wishes for your continued
success and wishing for you and for yours the
very best, I remain

Sincerely,

J. L. Plummer, Jr.

JLP/cwb

I had one man, Al Friedman who lived on the Beach, who called one year and wanted to take 100 golfers from his condominium to Freeport to play golf. We negotiated a rate and times but the group did not materialize. The next year Mr. Friedman called with the same request, I did the same work and again the group did not materialize. The third year Mr. Friedman called again and said "This is Al Friedman, do you remember me" I said "sure Mr. Friedman where don't you want to go this year?" He protested no, no he really had a group this year. And he did. We got a group of about 86 golfers to Freeport. Perseverance pays off.

I got a lead on a man named Jack Copenhaver who had an "in" with the Masonic Temples. He used to charter planes to take them to various destinations and also cruises. He gave me many charters for Masonic temples from a number of different cities. I also had a man named Dave Kurzband who was a junketteer. In other words he ran gambling charters and groups. This also led to other junketteers finding me to handle their groups. A junketteer had to hand pick his invitees as the casino operators watch every player who is brought in. If the player did not risk a certain amount of money he was not invited to go again. If the operator had too many of this type of player he was written off as a junketeer.

Besides Freeport we also had gambling groups to Aruba and Curacao and even to France using EASTERN from Miami to New York and Air France to Monaco. I once had a man from St. Maarten from the Concorde Hotel whose business card said Frankie Cee. I had heard the boys ran the casino there but I don't know. We could not make a deal.

The casino in Nassau wanted Eastern to fly their players over and back but the way they wanted the flights we would have lost money. They wanted a flight a 6:00 to 7:–pm and retrun at 2:00am. We would have to leave the plane out of service for 7 hours and have a double crew as the crew would not be legal for the return flight. Or we could ferry the plane back immediately then ferry another over for the return flight, much too costly. I must have turned them down a dozen times. .

Dave had a deal with the casino in Freeport and that led to meeting Albert Miller. Mr. Miller was, and I guess still is, the power behind Freeport. A former chief of Police in Nassau he was sent to Freeport to overlook the casino operations and many other things. We had to get him to sign off on any charter we did.

There was another man, Sam Fox, who was running a program called "The International Band Festival". The program was to send four high school bands to Mexico City and have them compete for the title of best band. The movement called for chartered airplanes to take the kids to Mexico City, which of course we were happy to supply. And the high school bands kids loved the trip, even if he did room them four to a room.

Ararat Temple

A.A.O.N.M.S.
300 WEST ELEVENTH STREET
KANSAS CITY, MISSOURI 64105
TELEPHONE 816-842-8888

GEORGE R. RHOADES
ILLUSTRIOUS POTENTATE

MILLARD D. HAMILTON
RECORDER

May 4, 1971

Mr. Lawrence C. Green, Manager Group Sales
Eastern Air Lines, Inc.
700 First National Bank Building
Miami, Florida 33131

Dear Mr. Green:

On behalf of the members of Ararat Temple will you please
accept our deep appreciation and thanks for all the courtesies
extended to our group at the Miami Airport last Saturday.
With your help we transported 247 people with a minimum of
confusion.

Once airborne the service was outstanding and Eastern Airlines
has our deep gratitude.

Very truly yours,

Millard D. Hamilton
Recorder

MDH:par

cc: Mr. Jack Copenhaver

114

Another source of revenue was the movement of children to summer camps in North Carolina and Georgia. We usually used regular scheduled airplanes rather than charters. The competition was amoung three airlines Eastern, Delta and Northwest. We all went after the camp owners or the travel agents who handled the groups. There was one group none of us weanted, handled by a Mrs. R. If I got the business the other two airline sales reps would call and laugh at me saying "ha, ha you got her this year" and I would do the same to them.

Someone had chosen Eastern to operate charters from Cuba to the United States to bring in refugees. Maybe because we had airplanes in Miami on hand and because we were so cooperative. They were usually last minute deals. I would get a call and go running to the FAA office at the airport with contracts for the charters.

I was in Freeport one time with a group of agents and we were invited to the Princess Towers for a reception. While I was there the sales manager of the hotel came over to me with another man in tow. The other man was an executive of the Sony Corporation from New Jersey. The two had a problem. The hotel man wanted the Sony's corporate meeting in his hotel and the Sony man wanted to do that also. The problem was to get all the Sony people into Freeport in one day and back out again when the meeting was over. There would be about 400 to 500 people at the meeting.

They asked if EASTERN would put on extra section or a bigger airplane to accommodate the group. I said no we would not as it took about a 70% load factor to breakeven on the flights. With 90% load factor going over and 10% coming back we would have only a 50% load factor on the round trip and we did not need the extra capacity. Then I thought of a way we might put on a bigger airplane. I asked the Sony man if I could get 2 L-1011 scheduled on the way over and 2 on the way back could he guarantee EASTERN could have all the business coming from around the country to Miami to connect with the Freeport flights. He said he could do that.

When I went back to Miami I got in touch with Mike Fenello who was Division Vice President Operational Coordination. Mike was a very good man, I had known him slightly at Idlewild when he was pilot flying the line. He said he would see if he could work it out and he did. We got a very big slice of revenue out of that movement. Mike was so well thought of that the FAA recruited him to go to work for them.

One of my first visits to Freeport with a group was when the Holiday Inn was first inaugurated. The resident manager was John McNeill. He was a Scot and if he were anymore of a Scot he wouldn't be able to talk at all. One evening about midnight we were all sitting around having a drink in the lounge and we heard this racket. We looked out and here was John coming down the hall in full kilt blowing his bagpipe. He was pretty good but I don't know how we all didn't get thrown out.

BLUE STAR'S SEVEN CAMPS
For Girls and Boys — In the Blue Ridge Mountains

HERMAN M. POPKIN
RODGER M. POPKIN
FOUNDER AND DIRECTORS

AFTER SEPT. 1ST
WINTER ADDRESS
3595 Sheridan St. Suite 206
Hollywood, Florida 33021
Broward: 305-963-4494
Dade: 305-624-2267

AFTER JUNE 1ST
SUMMER ADDRESS
Kanuga Road
P. O. Box 1029
Hendersonville, NC 28793
Phone: 704-692-3591

OUR 37TH SEASON — June 20 1984

Dear Mr. Green:

On behalf of our entire Blue Star family consisting of 700 campers and 300 staff, we want to express to you our sincere appreciation for all of the time and effort you put into helping us get our children to Camp safely last Sunday. We have received reports from our escorts that you and your personnel were exceedingly courteous and attentive to our children; that you did everything possible to see that they had an enjoyable and safe trip; and that they had as little difficulty as possible in reaching their destination. We are grateful and we wanted you to know how much we appreciated all that you did.

If ever you are in our area we hope you will come by for a visit. With every good wish, we are

Sincerely,

Herman & Rodger Popkin

Herman & Rodger Popkin

HP:lp

Mr. Larry C. Green
Vice President
Eastern Airlines
4890 NW 36th Street
Miami, FL 33148

ACCREDITED MEMBER
AMERICAN CAMPING ASSOCIATION

"A SUMMER
CAMPING ADVENTURE
WITH A PURPOSE"

117

John went on to do marketing for Holiday Inns in the Caribbean and then became a vice president for the Holiday Inn on Grand Cayman. He stayed there until they tore it down.

My first trip to the Laurentians Mountains was a fam trip Jim Pitts of Air Canada organized. At the airport in Montreal an immigrations inspector ask us where we were coming from, we were all wearing Miami Dolphin ski caps, we told him Miami and he said "you got to be out of your xxxx minds". We stayed at the Chalet Swiss in St Adele. Jim Pitts, Jim Connell, of the Miami Herald, and I had a very large triple room in a building that looked like a Swiss chalet, a beautiful place. Jim had gotten rental cars and we drove up from Montreal. I was one of the drivers since I knew how to drive in ice and snow. I guess it was turn about also as I had taken Jim on his first fam trip ever to Puerto Rico. I had him drive one of the vans we used. The van's horn did notwork so Jim stuck his hear out the wimdow and yelled "HONK".

We had a great time and I got to go skiing for the first time since I was 13. We also went snowmobiling at the hotel L'estreal the general manager, Jerry Lafontaine, there took us on a big lake and we ran all over the place. Then Jerry took us thru the woods and he was driving like a madman through the trees and brush, we had a hard time keeping up with him.

This started a love for the Laurentians in the Winter time. If you listened to the sales people from United and Braniff the only place to ski was Colorado or Utah (of course they flew there and not to Canada) They claimed the skiing was always icy in Canada which was not true. I took a group of agents up there every December for 5 or 6 years and every one loved it..

The first trip I ran was to the Laurentides Chalet in St Agape, about five miles North of St Adele. On the first night I arranged for a large sleigh to take the group for a night ride thru the countryside. Its absolutely beautiful night and most of the houses were already decorated for Christmas, it was just great

On the next day I took the group to the Swiss Chalet to get a taste of skiing. I had Fred and Francesca Merritt of the trip. Francesca was wearing a full length mink coat. We put the skis on Francesca and she promptly fell down. What a sight, a lady in a full length mink coat on her butt with the skis sticking up and unable to get up. There I had my first experience with a Palma lift and fell down the first time but got the hang of it after that.

We were invited for dinner at the Grey Rocks Hotel, near St. Jovite, and they put on a great dinner but the thing that impressed me most was at the end on the dinner they brought out a large cake with the Eastern logo on it. I was highly pleased.

On another trip to the Laurentians we stayed at the Chanti-clair Resort and I had scheduled a sleigh ride after dinner. Just before I went down for dinner I had a call from Archie, the activities director, and he asked if I still wanted to have the sleigh ride after dinner. I said, oh, yes why did he ask and he said it was 30 degrees below 0 outside. I said OH, paused for a minutes then said well we scheduled it lets go.

**SWISS CHALET
STE. ADELE, QUEBEC**

SWISS CHALET STE. ADELE, QUEBEC

**HOTEL CHANTECLER
STE. ADELE, QUEBEC**

We had a big sleigh pulled by two horses and a great big hairy blanket, which stunk to high heaven - but was warm, to cover us. But the thing that kept us warm though was the caribou (no not the animal) in French Canada caribou is a mixture of half red wine and half straight alcohol. The ride was beautiful and all enjoyed it. The only thing I regretted was when we returned I looked at the horses and they had ice cycles hanging from their mouths.

The next day we drove 40 miles up to St Jovite and we were greeted by the hotel people who asked "are you the nuts that went sleigh ridding last night in 30 below weather?". Yep that was us!

We used four or five different hotels on these trips, one being the Villa Bellvue near St Jovite not far from Mount Tremblant. The hotel would outfit us with boots and skis then bus us over to Mount Tremblant for skiing. On one of these trips an agent took a picture of me all decked out with my Dolphin hat on ready to get on the bus back to the hotel. (See Picture)

Another time they took us cross country skiing in a preserve run by some order of Christian brothers. It was a pristine land-scape and a refuge for birds. The guide had brought bird seed with him and told us to put some on the palm of our hand and hold it up. Then the birds would come down and eat right out of our hands. I got to tell you in cross country skiing you really find new muscles or one you hadn't used in a long time, but it was worth it.

One of the travel agent groups (1976) I took was to the Chantecler Hotel in St Adele. They had their own ski runs and we didn't have to take a bus to the run, but could be out on the slopes in a few minutes. The Chantecler also had a real fine dining room with magnificent food. The next year (1977) I took an interline group up to the same place and they had a ball. (See pictures) On that trip we also went snowmobiling at the Hotel L'Estoreal. Johnny and Rita Perez had a machine that wouldn't go and the ranger gave them his, after that we couldn't keep up with Johnny. I had Frankie Wiills on the back of mine and she leaned the wrong way and over we went but we got the hang of it real quick. We also had lunch over at Cuttles, a very charming place with a big roaring fire place and Berta Palacio played, very well, the piano for us.

Jim Pitts arranged to take a group up to the Winter Carnival in Quebec one year. As we were driving into the city we passed the Plains of Abraham and I flashed back to the old history lesson of the French and English war with Generals Montcalm and Wolfe fighting for the whole of Canada, which the British won in 1759. The city has built a presentation in a theater across the street from the Chateau Frontenac on how the battle was won.

We stayed at the Chateau Frontenac, an old grand dame of a hotel and still wonderful, right on a hill top over looking the St Laurence River. My roommate was Gib Gibbons who was the reservation manger for Eastern in Miami. The hotel had set up an ice rink and tobaggan run next to the hotel. The tobaggan was real fun and we would do it a number of times. Jim Pitts was a riot on the ice skates as he had never been on them before but he survived the ordeal.

Also next to the hotel was an inclinator that took us down to the old town of Quebec which is now a museum, The old city was right on the banks of the St Lawrence River. We ate in a few of the fine restaurants in Quebec and they were excellent..

Some people may ask where I got the time to take these and other trips. I used my vacation days. I had 25 years seniority in 1973 and had 25 days vacation. I would split up the days and take a Friday or Monday coupled with the weekends, some times Friday and Mondays I hardly ever took a whole weeks vacation. I also worked 10 hours a day from 8:30am/8:45am to 6:30pm. Most times it was just myself asd Luis Palacio in the office at 6:30pm.

In 1971 I joined the Travel Industry Association of Florida (TIA) which was the largest travel association in Miami. Most of the owners and managers of the travel agencies belonged plus some airline and cruiseline people. I was elected to the board of directors and served in various positions including program chairman. As such we had Spain for the sponsor one time and I got the Flamenco Restaurant on the 79th Street Causeway for the evening. That was the biggest turn out we ever had with about 300 attendees. I was elected president for the year of 1976/77. We also took TIA on some fam trips to San Francisco, Santiago, Chile, Guatemala, Panama, Buenos Aires and even Yugoslavia (Eastern to New York, you know).

I took a weeks vacation in 1982 and took the travel agents to Yugoslavia. It was a great trip. The people were all very friendly and down to earth. They liked Tito because although he was a communist he kept the Russian communists out of Yugoslavia and ran the country as a socialist state. That means the government did not own all the business. You could have a private business but after 7 employees you had to run the company as a cooperative.

We flew Eastern (naturally) to New York and JAT to Belgrade, Yugoslavia. We had to hustle to catch the plane to Dubrovnik. When we checked into the hotel (the Libertas) we had to go down to the rooms as the hotel was built on the side of a hill that sloped into the Adriatic Sea, giving everyone a beautiful view of the Sea. WE spent two nights in Dubrovnik, visiting the old city and it was special, with the old walls and towers. A couple of us rented a car and drove to Mustar, which is where ruminants of the Turkish army settled after their defeat. It was a city with minarets and mosques. We had lunch in an inn that overlooked the Nereiva River with an old bridge over it that was over 800 years old. It was a narrow bridge for foot or horse traffic, very picturesque. In the Bosnian war one side blew it up just out of meanness. (See picture)

THE 800 YEAR OLD BRIDGE, DESTROYED IN THE BOSNIAN WAR

FORMERLY A FISHING VILLAGE, NOW IT IS ONE HOTEL

The next day we were taken to another hotel down the coast to Igalo. The town was a spa town where they were claiming all sorts of health improvements. The Plaza Hotel was new and very modern. That night they had a dinner for us in an inn up on the hillside and they went all out with a great time. We had cocktails (cocktails? that slivervitz really packs a wallop.) first then dinner by a big roaring fire place. They even brought in musicians to play for us.

After that we returned to Belgrade and stayed two nights at the Metropol Hotel. Belgrade is located at the convergence of the Sava and Danube rivers and they have built a large modern convention center on the banks of the Sava River called, what else?, the Sava Center. On the last night we had the farewell dinner at the Skadarlija restaurant in a private room. During the dinner they brought in various musical groups that go from restaurant to restaurant playing for the guest. They were great and a good ending to a wonderful trip.

In 1985 we had another trip to Yugoslavia and it was equally as wonderful as the first trip. This time we flew to Zagreb on JAT and over nighted there. Then we drove North thru Ljubljana to Lake Bled and over nighted there. The lake has Austria on the North and Yugoslavia on the South and is as picturesque as any lake in the World. From there we entered the Plitvice Forest and spent one night there. The Forest is a nature preserve and absolutely beautiful. There are 16 emerald green lakes that cascade into one another. In the middle of the forest is a very nice hotel. On a tour of the forest our guide ran off and left half the group in the forest. We joined the Fuquari Indian tribe to find our way out.

From there we went to Split for one night and on to Dubrovnik for two nights. While at Dubrovnik we visited Sveti Stefan, which used to be a fishing village and now the whole island has been turned into a hotel using various houses as guest rooms. We followed around the Bay of Kotor, which is really a long curving fjord, with deep water all the way to the city of Kotor which is a medieval town architecturally interesting. I hope all the wars have left these places in tact.

We returned to Zagreb for the flight to New York but there were mechanical problems with the airplane so JAT worked out a flight on Lufthansa to London and Pan Am to New York. Before we could get on the plane JAT had another itinerary using a brand new JAT plane to London and Pan Am to New York. We got to London in good in good shape and realized if we took the Pan Am flight to New York we would have to overnight in New York. Someone suggested we take Eastern to Miami instead. We would have to overnight in England but figured it was worth it as once we were on we would be home. The one problem was no pass riders or travel agent fam trips were allowed to fly that route. Here is where Charley Scully came to our rescue and authorized our passage. We made our way from Heathrow to Gatwick and over nighted there. Eastern, as a newcomer, was not allowed to fly into Heathrow which had all the connecting flights to Europe. It worked out fine for us without having to make two connection to get home.

Plitvicka Forest, Mercy & Wally Bithorn, Silvia Forcino, Ruth Fiengold Doris
Jordan, Ruby Levin. behind the sign Linda Nichols, Linda Collins, Marlene
& Walter Feteke, Aliza Brenner, kneelimg Heather Lambert and Larry

City of Kotar on the Bay of Kotar

In 1984 I took the members of TIA to Buenos Aires. We stayed at the Plaza Hotel right at the head of Florida Street, the main shopping street in the city. The Plaza is now the Marriott and we couldn't afford the price now. We took the group out to El Mangrullo for lunch and to see a Gaucho show. (See picture)

The Travel Industry Association held an annual SKI-FAIR for nineteen years starting 1981. The first ten years it was a big show and then it dwindled down. We had 80 to 100 booths and about 800 to 1,000 people attended for the first few years. Carol Morse was in charge of getting the ski suppliers signed up and assigning the booths. (A really big job) and I was in charge of getting the place, doing the layout and ordering the catering. We used the largest ballroom in the Omni Hotel on Biscayne Blvd for the few years. After Carol moved out of town Eileen Huber took over the job of getting the suppliers. In the first few years we had agents from all over Miami, Ft Lauderdale, West Palm Beach, the Keys, Naples and George Munro, the Eastern sales manager from Savannah, even made a two day fam trip out of it. He brought about 15 travel agents with him and they stayed at the Omni Hotel. His agents were very pleased with the trip. The agents in Miami sold many ski trips as a results of these shows.

Come To The Fair . . South Florida Ski Fair '88

A joint effort of the entire South Florida travel community.

SEPTEMBER 29, 1988 AT THE OMNI HOTEL
1601 Biscayne Boulevard
Miami, Florida

TIA's 7th annual **SKI FAIR** promises to be the best yet! The biggest ski show available **only** to the South Florida travel industry.

All of your favorite ski properties and services, tour operators, airlines and car rental companies will be there with their new Winter 88/89 promotions.

INCORPORATED 1985

**THE TRAVEL INDUSTRY
ASSOCIATION OF FLORIDA**

Over 60 suppliers will be on hand from Europe, Colorado, Utah, Wyoming, Montana, Canada, California, New England, North Carolina and Nevada to bring you up to date on their services. Come meet them, greet them and ply them with questions.

*A tax deductible donation of
$3 per person will be collected at the door.
All proceeds will go to the U.S. Olympic Ski Team.
Complimentary food and beverages will be available.
Show hours from 5:30 p.m. to 9:00 p.m.*

Don't Miss SKI FAIR '88

FILL IN THIS FORM AND MAIL IT TODAY!

We are coming to SKI FAIR '88 at the Omni Hotel in Miami, Florida on September 29, 1988. Registration starts at 5:30 p.m.

Please type or print:

Name: _____ Number Attending: _____

Agency: _____

Address: _____ City: _____

State / Country: _____ Zip Code: _____

132

Travel Weekly November 1982
Travel Industry Association Ski Fair at the Omni Hotel
Eastern Airlines Booth note "We have your mountain" poster
Larry Green, Sandi Cesaretti-Eastern Airlines sales rep, the Bonne Homme,
symbol of Quebec's Winter Carnival and Jim Negron-Third Century Tours

Various people were in charge of the program that preceded the trade show. About the third year I asked to do the program. I wrote the script for the program where I identified each of the ski areas and showed the hotels, facilities and attractions in each of the areas. I got Freddie Blackwell to be the narrator and he was excellent as usual. I asked Elliott Trotta, who was Manager of corporate presentations for Eastern to do the slides and movie. Elliot out did himself and made as outstanding program. I have never seen a better ski presentation.

When Andrew hit in 1992 it caused many people to move to West Broward county. The traffic became unbearable and many agents stopped going to any kind of promotion. All the evening meeting organizations dwindled down to fifty people or less. The SKI-Fair was canceled that year and the number of suppliers and attendees became less and less so TIA ceased the program in 1999.

When I was downtown I got to know a number of people including representatives from various tourist offices. The Cayman Islands had an office in the First National Bank also. I got to know David Richardson the manager and we would talk. One day he asked me how he could get a brochure on the Cayman Islands that was sponsored by an airline. He wanted this because if he had an inclusive tour brochure the travel agents could earn 10% instead of the normal 7%. Nearly all the Caribbean destinations had inclusive tour brochures. I told him he needed an IT (inclusive tour) number in order for the agents to claim 10%. EASTERN was not then flying into the Caymans and Cayman Air was not in existence. I figured if I put together an EASTERN brochure the Cayman Islands would pay for it and distribute it then we would have our name linked to the Caymans and get more exposure for EASTERN. So I put the first IT brochure together to sell the Cayman Islands, we used Eastern to the gateway (Miami) and Lacsa Airlines to Grand Cayman. (See brochure).

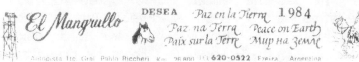

Gaucho, Gene Stevens, Gloria Risech, Art Horwitz, Maria Yuque, Susanne Norlem, Jackie DiBernardo, ?, Wally Bithorn
Larry, Eileen Purisch, Donna Fishel, Liz Toro, Heidi Bruni, ?, ?, Mercy Bithorn, Valerie Walker, BIG Gaucho
Kaye Weathers, ?, ?, Heather Lambert

I also set up the first Eastern Airlines/ Holiday Inns brochure. Mike Pico was the regional manager for Holidays Inns in the Caribbean. They had properties in many of the Caribbean Islands and he wanted to put together an IT brochure with Eastern Airlines. I took him to see Jim McEntegart, who was in charge of the brochures for Eastern. Jim like the program but did not want to do it. Jim said to me go ahead and do it yourself - so I did. I worked it out on I 6" by 9" Eastern brochure shell with only 3 hotels, the one in Jamaica, one in Nassau and one in Freeport, I believe these were chosen because Holiday Inn owned them and the rest were franchises. This became Holiday Inn Sun Spree Vacations. The home office took it over after two years. Then it became an 8" by 9" many page brochure with all the Holiday Inns in the Caribbean. I guess Holidays Inns liked the name because now they call some of their hotels Sun Spree hotels.

Holiday Inns INC. 3796 LAMAR AVENUE MEMPHIS TENNESSEE 38118 U.S.A. 9C

April 9, 1973

Mr. Larry Green
Eastern Airlines
700 First National Bank Building
Miami, Florida

Dear Larry:

Enclosed please find photocopies on the remaining four, four-color consumer package brochures displaying Eastern Airlines IT numbers that we are developing for various Holiday Inn resorts this summer.

We certainly appreciate you processing our primary package brochure relative to IT numbers through Mike Picot a few weeks ago.

The enclosed brochures, which I'm sure Mike has previously discussed with you, cover our Honeymoon, Golf, Tennis, Family and Maxi and Mini packages for Holiday Inn resorts this summer. These photocopies are much smaller than the actual size of the borchure (4" x 9" per panel) when printed. Please let me know if there is any additional information you need on this promotional material relative to IT number approval. I will forward press-proofs just as soon as they are available.

Cordially,

Tom Meeks
Director
Regional Sales and Promotion

cc: Mick Picot

Enclosure

TAM/bjm

137

Fly to
Jamaica or the Bahamas

OUT OF THE ORDINARY POST CONVENTION TOURS... AT OUT OF THE ORDINARY HOLIDAY INNS

After the Convention

Why not relax a little, laze in the sunshine and let the gentle breezes caress away your cares and tensions.

Visit an out of the ordinary Holiday Inn in Jamaica or the Bahamas. Each luxurious resort Inn has its own private beach, where you can skin and scuba dive, sport fish, ski or sail a catamaran. Championship 18 hole golf courses are available nearby, tennis and horseback riding. For the ladies, there are shopping and sightseeing tours with duty free bargains galore.

Dine beneath the stars, sample the gourmet delights of traditional island dishes, swing with both island and international entertainment or dice with Lady Luck in the Casino.

Island Frolic I
3 Days / 2 Nights

Package Includes:

Personal meeting service	Complimentary tennis
Assistance through Customs	Complimentary cruise
Transportation to Inn	lounges & towels
Luxurious accommodations	Daily activity programme
Hotel taxes	Gratuities—maids,
Shoppers bonus book	pool & bellboys
Welcome rum cocktail	Return transportation
party	to airport

138

Holiday Inn, Freeport, Grand Bahama Island

Relax a little — enjoy an island frolic at Freeport's out of the ordinary Holiday Inn — located on the beach — with the fishing fleet and underwater explorers club a short stroll away. You can skin and scuba dive — sport fish — ski — or sail a catamaran. Enjoy our 4 match play tennis courts, or take up the challenge of the 3 18-hole championship golf courses nearby. At night, 'neath tropic skies, feast on sumptuous island delicacies or dice with Lady Luck at the Casino

Holiday Inn, Paradise Island, Nassau

Paradise is out of the ordinary — and so is our Holiday Inn. Framed by swaying pines on Pirates Cove, the tallest Inn in the Bahamas offers an unsurpassed vista of island beauty. After a day filled with water sports, golf, sunshine and leisure, dine and dance to island rhythms with international entertainment in the Crow's Nest supper club, and maybe later, gamble at Black Jack or Roulette at the nearby Paradise Island Casino.

Holiday Inn, Montego Bay, Jamaica

Luxuriant hills, coursed by sparkling streams, create a dramatic background for Jamaica's out of the ordinary Holiday Inn, situated on a lazy curve of the beach in the old Rose Hall Plantation Estate near Montego Bay. A round of golf — tennis — fishing — maybe the Great House tour — or a rafting trip down the Martha Brae will whet your appetite for the Inn's nighttime pleasures. Dine at the "Oasis Grill" or the Plantation Room, and later join the Inn crowd and thrill to both island and international entertainment in the "Witches Hideaway."

Island Frolic I   3 Days / 2 Nights

Holiday Inn, Freeport, Grand Bahama Island

Apr. 9 - Dec. 16, 1972 IT2EA1HIF1	Double	Single	Third Person
Rates Per Person	$28.00	$44.00	$25.00
Extra Night	9.50	17.00	8.00
Dec. 17 - Apr. 28, 1973 IT2EA1HIF2			
Rates Per Person	$44.00	$76.00	$38.00
Extra Night	17.00	32.00	14.00

Holiday Inn, Paradise Island, Nassau

Apr. 9 - Dec. 16, 1972 IT2EA1HIP1	Double	Single	Third Person
Rates Per Person	$34.00	$54.00	$31.00
Extra Night	11.50	21.00	10.00
Dec. 17 - Apr. 28, 1973 IT2EA1HIP2			
Rates Per Person	$44.00	$76.00	$38.00
Extra Night	17.00	32.00	14.00

Holiday Inn, Montego Bay, Jamaica

Apr. 9 - Dec. 20, 1972 IT2EA1HIJ1	Double	Single	Third Person
Rates Per Person	$34.00	$48.00	$30.00
Extra Night	13.00	20.00	11.00
Dec. 21 - Apr. 28, 1973 IT2EA1HIJ2			
Rates Per Person	$55.00	$74.00	$45.00
Extra Night	23.00	32.00	18.00

Island Frolic II   3 Days / 2 Nights

Holiday Inn, Freeport, Grand Bahama Island

Apr. 9 - Dec. 16, 1972 IT2EA1HIF3	Double	Single	Third Person
Rates Per Person	$54.00	$82.00	$60.00
*Extra Night	20.50	28.00	19.00
Dec. 17 - Apr. 28, 1973 IT2EA1HIF4			
Rates Per Person	$77.00	$113.00	$70.00
*Extra Night	28.00	43.00	25.00

Holiday Inn, Paradise Island, Nassau

Apr. 9 - Dec. 16, 1972 IT2EA1HIP3	Double	Single	Third Person
Rates Per Person	$70.00	$93.00	$66.00
*Extra Night	22.50	32.00	21.00
Dec. 17 - Apr. 28, 1973 IT2EA1HIP4			
Rates Per Person	$83.00	$119.00	$76.00
*Extra Night	28.00	43.00	25.00
*Extra Night rate includes breakfast & dinner.			

Holiday Inn, Montego Bay, Jamaica

Apr. 9 - Dec. 16, 1972 IT2EA1HIJ3	Double	Single	Third Person
Rates Per Person	$68.00	$84.00	$64.00
*Extra Night	24.00	31.00	22.00
Dec. 21 - Apr. 28, 1973 IT2EA1HIJ4			
Rates Per Person	$93.00	$113.00	$82.00
*Extra Night	35.00	44.00	30.00

Due to U.S. dollar devaluation, the above rates are subject to local currency exchange rates.

I also worked out a program with John Zimmerman who worked for Holland American Cruise Lines. John asked me if I would help him get some business out of South Florida, Holland America did not come into Miami or Ft Lauderdale at that time. He had a ship, the SS Statendam, sailing from New York to Bermuda and we set up a program for those trips. We produced a brochure on an Eastern Bermuda shell and it did produce additional revenue for both Eastern and Holland America. John and I remained friends until he retired. Incidently I can't tell you how wonderful the people in EASTERN's print shop were. I did quite a few brochures and they were marvelous with their help and suggestions. And they always delivered a quality product on time. I wish I could remember their names.

FLY/FLOAT

Bermuda

Cruise schedule
from New York

New York Saturdays	New York Saturdays
Dep. 6 p.m.*	Arr. 8 a.m.
Apr. 19	Apr. 26
Apr. 26	May 3
May 3	May 10
May 10	May 17
May 17	May 24
May 24	May 31
May 31	Jun. 7
Jun. 7	Jun. 14
Jun. 14	Jun. 21
Aug. 30	Sep. 6
Sep. 6	Sep. 13
Sep. 13	Sep. 20
Sep. 20	Sep. 27
Sep. 27	Oct. 4
Oct. 4	Oct. 11
Oct. 11	Oct. 18
Oct. 18	Oct. 25
Oct. 25	Nov. 1
Nov. 1	Nov. 8
Nov. 8	Nov. 15
Nov. 15	Nov. 22
Nov. 22	Nov. 29

EASTERN

14-PF-0181   2/70   100M Printed in U.S.A.

FLY TO NEW YORK

VIA

EASTERN AIRLINES

CRUISE

TO

BERMUDA

VIA

HOLLAND-AMERICAN

S. S. STATENDAM

SEVEN DAYS

CRUISE
PRICES FROM
$565⁰⁰ to $610⁰⁰

**PER PERSON,
DOUBLE OCCUPANCY
DELUXE OUTSIDE CABIN
2 LOWER BEDS**
PLUS AIR FARE

CHOOSE ANY EASTERN AIRLINES FLIGHT
AND HOLLAND AMERICAN CRUISES WILL
RETURN $145 TOWARD YOUR AIR FARE.
NO RESTRICTIONS, NO SPECIAL DAYS OF
TRAVEL. TICKET GOOD FOR ONE YEAR.

Typical accommodations

Deluxe One-Room Suites
bath and shower

Two windows in these luxurious one-room
suites comprising sleeping area with twin
beds, bath and shower. Separate sitting
area where you can entertain your friends.
Located on Upper Promenade deck.

Deluxe Outside Staterooms
bath and shower

Luxury two-porthole stateroom with sea
view. Twin beds, all bathroom facilities.
Room enough for an impromptu cocktail
party. Located on Main and A decks with
some on Upper Promenade and C decks.

142

I worked out some packages to the Bahamas with Harold Binder of Wyllys Tours that were unique. One package was a one night stay in Nassau and the other a one day trip over in the morning and back in the afternoon.

I was always interested in getting business from the cruise lines. I could see that cruising would become a major source of revenue for Eastern Airlines. I set up some of the first air/sea programs with Royal Caribbean and with Monarch Cruise Lines. With Royal Caribbean they had ten days cruises that were not doing too well and we worked out a program where we would fly the passengers to St Thomas, missing the first days of the cruise and returning by ship to Miami. On the other hand we would fly passengers from St Thomas back to Miami after they had completed the cruise from Miami. We had the Columbus Hotel Ticket office issue all the tickets and Isadore, their porter would take them to the cruiseline. We were selling $25,000.00 to $40,000.00 a month with this program.

July 17, 1974

Ms. Linda Perez
Royal Caribbean Tours
903 South America Way
Miami, Florida

Dear Linda:

Enclosed are the invoices for May and June.

The invoices for May total $25,050.71 and for June
$32,050.55. May we please have your check for both
amounts as soon as possible?

Thank you for the business and we look forward to
being of help to you.

Sincerely,

L. C. Green
Manager/Agency Sales

LCG:ns

Encls.

144

April 27, 1977

Mr. Philip Terrano
Manager Air/Sea
Monarch Cruise Lines
1428 Brickell Avenue
Miami, Florida 33131

Dear Philip:

We have confirmed the space you requested for the holiday period.

10 Seats from	Birmingham	on 891 on Dec. 18, 19, 26	
10 Seats to	Birmingham	on 894 on Dec. 26, Jan. 1, 2	
10 Seats from	Charlotte	on 729 on Dec. 18, 19, 26	
10 Seats to	Charlotte	on 726 on Dec. 26, Jan. 1, 2	
10 Seats from	Hartford	on 181 on Dec. 18, 19, 26	
10 Seats to	Hartford	on 182 on Dec. 26, Jan. 1, 2	
10 Seats from	Raleigh-Durham	on 863 on Dec. 18, 19, 26	
10 Seats to	Raleigh-Durham	on 898 on Dec. 26, Jan. 1, 2	

The times of these flights will be adjusted seasonally on the December schedule. That time of year, is of course, peak season so be sure the peak season ticketing rules are conformed to.

I thank you for the business and would sure like to get a piece of the New York business since we have a far superior schedule than any other airline.

Sincerely,

L. C. Green
Manager Agency Sales

LCG:ncs

I went over to talk with Bob Dickenson at Carnival Cruise Lines when their office was on Biscayne Blvd and 7th Street. They only had a couple of ships at that time but I was trying to get some of the airline business bringing passengers into Miami. After we talked I brought the information to Chuck Kramer, a vice president for Eastern Airlines, but his opinion was that Carnival was trying to get us to buy the business. I explained that all they wanted was help with the advertising and such. We did not make a deal but two years later Eastern was frantically chasing the cruise business.

CAYMAN ISLANDS TOURIST BOARD

125 S. E. THIRD AVENUE • MIAMI, FLORIDA 33131
TELEPHONE: (Area Code 305) 358-0608

August 18, 1971

Mr. Larry Green, Group Manager
Eastern Air Lines, Inc.
700 First National Bank Building
100 Biscayne Blvd.
Miami, Florida   33132

Dear Larry:

I want to formally express my appreciation for your
invaluable assistance with our package programme.

For your ready information I enclose a copy of the
finished product.

With kind personal regards,

David E. Richardson
General Sales Manager

Encl.

DER/r

Fly Eastern

SAMPLE ROUND TRIP EXCURSION JET FARES**

FROM:

NEW YORK	$183.00
BALTIMORE	178.00
PHILADELPHIA	183.00
CHICAGO	199.00
DETROIT	196.00
ATLANTA	164.44
WASHINGTON	178.00
CLEVELAND	196.00
MIAMI	70.00

Air fares subject to change without notice.

Change planes in Miami** to Lacsa Airlines for non-stop service to Grand Cayman. Baggage can be checked through to destination.

**21 day excursion plus tax, available to November 30, 1971.

RATES EFFECTIVE: AUG. 1, 1971 to Dec. 15, 1971

Litho in U.S.A. 8/71

on

Grand Cayman Island

EASTERN The Wings of Man

GREATER THAN GRAND

... is Grand Cayman, a gem of tropical loveliness situated just a short flight south of Miami, and west of Jamaica. One of the still delightfully quiet islands of the Caribbean, Grand Cayman specializes in poolside relaxation, exciting skin diving and water sports, glorious beaches and the friendliest folk to be found anywhere. Choice resort accommodations range from plush luxury to more rustic island-type, with superb cuisine and sparkling cleanliness. Shopping is fun and inexpensive at freeport shops in the hotels and Georgetown, and sightseeing along beachfront roads and quaint country lanes is different here than anywhere else. Peaceful, tropical and beauful, Grand Cayman is a delightful change of place, for a delightful vacation!

CAYMAN ISLAND HOLIDAYS

PER PERSON RATES EFFECTIVE: Aug. 1, 1971 to Dec. 15, 1971
MEAL PLANS AS INDICATED

4 DAYS - 3 NIGHTS IT-1-EA-1-C300

Hotel	Plan	Acc.	Single	Double	Triple	Extra Nights Single	Extra Nights Double	Extra Nights Triple
BEACH CLUB COLONY (Full Breakfast)	CP	Std	42.50	39.00	36.05	12.50	12.00	11.35
		Mod	51.00	43.50	39.05	15.00	13.50	12.35
		Sup	60.00	48.00	42.05	18.00	15.00	13.35
CARIBARTEL APARTMENT HOTEL (5)	EP	Apt.	83.50	41.75	32.85	25.00	12.50	10.00
CARIBBEAN CLUB LTD. (8)	MAP	Ocean Villa	128.00	72.25	63.30	40.00	22.75	20.20
		Colony Villa	110.00	62.50	56.70	34.00	19.50	18.00
DRIFTWOOD VILLAGE (Cottages only) (1)	EP	Std.	—	30.00	25.05	—	10.00	8.35
GALLEON BEACH (2)	MAP	Std	87.50	57.75	54.55	20.60	18.00	17.35
LA FONTAINE HOTEL (4)	MAP	Sup	68.00	58.00	48.75	20.00	18.00	15.35
RUM POINT CLUB (5) (6) (7)	MAP	Std	91.00	68.00	65.35	25.00	20.00	20.00
TORTUGA CLUB (2) (3)	AP	Std	60.00	52.50	45.00	20.00	17.50	15.00

7 DAYS - 6 NIGHTS IT-1-EA-1-C301

Hotel	Plan	Acc.	Single	Double	Triple	Extra Nights Single	Extra Nights Double	Extra Nights Triple
BEACH CLUB COLONY (Full Breakfast)	CP	Std	81.00	75.00	70.10	12.50	12.00	11.35
		Mod	96.00	84.00	76.10	15.00	13.50	12.35
		Sup	114.00	93.00	82.10	18.00	15.00	13.35
CARIBARTEL APARTMENT HOTEL (5)	EP	Apt.	158.50	79.25	62.85	25.00	12.50	10.00
CARIBBEAN CLUB LTD. (8)	MAP	Ocean Villa	248.00	140.00	123.90	40.00	22.75	20.20
		Colony Villa	212.00	121.00	110.70	34.00	19.50	18.00
DRIFTWOOD VILLAGE (Cottages only) (1)	EP	Std	—	60.00	50.10	—	10.00	8.35
GALLEON BEACH (2)	MAP	Std	127.50	111.75	108.60	20.00	18.00	17.35
LA FONTAINE HOTEL (4)	MAP	Sup	128.00	112.00	94.80	20.00	18.00	15.35
RUM POINT CLUB (5) (6) (7)	MAP	Std	166.00	136.00	125.35	25.00	20.00	20.00
TORTUGA CLUB (2) (3)	AP	Std	120.00	105.00	90.00	20.00	17.50	15.00

5% Government tax collected directly by hotel.
(1) Standard rate rooms not air conditioned.
(2) 10% service charge added to bill in lieu of gratuities.
(3) Two children up to age 6 sharing room with parents free including meals.
(4) One child 12 or under sharing room with parents $5.00 MAP. Two children 12 or under sharing room with parents $10.00 MAP.
(5) Children's rates upon request.
(6) 15% service charge added to bill in lieu of gratuities.
(7) Round trip transfer airport/dock by taxi and dock to Rum Point by boat.
(8) 10% service charge on accommodations. 15% service charge on food and bar added to bill in lieu of gratuities.

INCLUDES: 1. Round trip transfers from airport to hotel of your choice. **2.** Room with private bath on meal plan as specified at hotel of your choice.

OPTIONAL CAR RENTAL: (CICO Rent-a-car system, an Avis affiliate) RATES: **$12** daily, weekly rates available.
Car rentals cannot be delivered to airport on arrival but will be delivered to your hotel. Therefore, transfer included in the tour must be used. On departure, car may be left at airport or your hotel. Models Available: Ford Escorts, Austin 100's, Mini Mokes, Volkswagens, Ford Cortinas, Pink Lady Jeeps. Rate Includes: Unlimited mileage, maintenance, insurance (100% liability $1 per day additional).

I was friendly with Segundo Fernandez who owned Fergis Travel. He had a deal with Royal Caribbean to ticket all their cruise passengers flying into Miami. We used to have lunch from time to time and Eastern was able to pick up a lot of revenue from Segundo. Segundo was a very nice man.

I was also friends with Wes Spencer, who I knew from his days with Northwest Airlines. He started an agency. with Joe Haber. called Universal Tours and he managed to get all the Norwegian Caribbean business. We got a lot of business from them also. We placed teleticketing machines in Universal and many of the tickets were received by this method. That was the first stage of automating travel agencies. Wes died early and his sister took over the business but she and NCL did not get along. This ended with NCL taking all their business in house. Now, of course, all the cruiselines have their own air/sea departments. Naturally this became big business and the executive office decided they would handle all the cruise lines.

About that time the First National Bank had an idea to distribute airline tickets thru their drive thru windows at their branch on NW 36th Street just west of Le Jeune Road. I worked to get them a teleticketing machine set up in that office and we had it for a few years but it was not a big success and we dropped the program.

Durning this time I continued to operate interline fam trips and went on a few (quite a few). I produced an interline brochure in 1970,1971,1972,1973, 1974 and the prices are something that are hard to believe. The brochures were all 4 panels but my scanner couldn't fit in but three so in the 1970 brochure had Freeport, at $32.00 left off, the 1971 has St Croix, at $42.00 left off, and the 1974 had Antigua, at $65.00 left off. The brochures were hand made by me, the print shop would not turn out anything as tacky as I did, but the brochures worked. See the copies of the brochures and the prices. (I couldn't find the 1973 brochure, guess we used them all up). We ran quite a number of trips as you see and carried a big number of interline people and made a lot of friends for Eastern. In 1975 I had too much going on to operate many interline trips or make a full brochure. I did however run trips whenever I had the opportunity in 1975,1976 and 1977. After deregulation set in the airlines were not as friendly with each other and I became more involved with the travel agents. With that happening the trips I did then were for travel agents to the Caribbean, Mexico, Central and South America, Canada, New York and San Francisco.

In 1975 I received the award of "Interline Man of the Year" distinction for 1974 as selected by the Miami Interline Club. I guess I ran more interline trips than any one else and I covered a lot of airlines and airline people. I also think Lou Palacio had something to do with my getting the award.

The Civil Aeronautics Board was out in 1978 and deregulation was in. And disaster was in for the finest airline system in the World. We were the envy of all the countries with lower air fares than Europe, for example to fly from London to Paris was almost three times as much as from New York to Washington. There was not much of a change for the first few years except for some airlines trying to fly everywhere in the World. Braniff Airlines expanded too fast and went broke. As a result Eastern was able to buy the South American routes from Braniff.

ST. CROIX

$34.00

TOUR DATES: May 22-24, Oct. 9-11, Oct.16-18.

Three days, two nights $34.00 per person in double room. Single room higher.

FRIDAY

Check in one hour prior to Eastern flight at the Miami Airport. On arrival you will be transported to the lovely ESTATE CARLTON. Afternoon free for a swim in the pool. That evening a welcome party given by Mr.Bachman, General Manager, followed by dinner on the patio.

SATURDAY

Breakfast on the patio, after which you will be taken to Christiansted for a boat trip to Buck Island. Here swimming, snorkeling and an under-sea trail prevails. After the boat trip, you will be free to shop in Christiansted. Dinner that night at the hotel.

SUNDAY

Breakfast at your leisure. Morning free until then-thirty at which time you will be taken to Davis Bay Beach for cocktails and beach barbecue, courtesy Virgin Islands Department of Commerce. Back to the hotel at three-thirty and prepare for trip back to Miami.

CONDITIONS

EASTERN

⬯ EASTERN

INTERLINE TOURS
1970

NASSAU

$26.00

DATES: June 5-7, Sept. 18-20, Sept. 25-27.

days, two nights $26.00 per person in
le room. Single room higher.

FRIDAY

in one hour prior to your Eastern
t to Nassau. Upon arrival in Nassau you
be transferred to the beautiful
RAL HOTEL. After check-in, everyone into
suits for transportation to the
RAL'S private island and a cocktail
. Dinner that night will be at the
RAL. The evening will be free.

SATURDAY

fast in the dining room at your leisure.
est of the day will be free except
will be served at the hotel. That
ng cocktails courtesy of the Bahama
try of Tourism, followed by dinner in
ining room. The evening will be free
you to explore the night life of Nassau
aradise Beach.

SUNDAY

fast at the hotel at your leisure and
will also be at the hotel. Time for
t minute swim or shopping at the straw
t, transfer back to the airport and

COZUMEL

$39.00

TOUR DATES: May 16-19, Oct.24-27, Nov.14-17.

Four days, three nights $39.00 per person in
double room. Single room higher.

SATURDAY

Check in one hour prior to Mexicana flight
from Miami. Flight courtesy of Mexicana
Airlines. On arrival in Cozumel you will be
transferred to the HOTEL MARA (May 16),
CANTARELL (Oct. 24), or PLAYA AZUL (Nov. 14).
Dinner at your hotel.

SUNDAY

Breakfast at your leisure. The day will be
free to roam around the town of San Miguel
or for a swim. Lunch and dinner at the
hotel.

MONDAY

Breakfast at the hotel, then all set for a
Robinson Caruso trip by boat to San Francisco
Beach. Lunch will be a picnic lunch at the
beach. Dinner at the hotel.

TUESDAY

Breakfast at the hotel, then transfer to
airport for return trip via Mexicana
Airlines.

BE SURE TO GET MEXICAN TOURIST CARD.

SAN JUAN

$35.00

TOUR DATES: Apr.30-May 3,Sept.10-13,Sept.18-20

Four days, three nights $35.00 per person in
double room. Single room higher.

THURSDAY

Check in one hour prior to Eastern flight
from Miami. On arrival in San Juan, reception
by the Department of Tourism. Then transfer
to FLAMBOYAN HOTEL. That evening cocktails
and dinner.

FRIDAY

After breakfast, a drive out to the Dorado
Beach Hotel and the Dorado Hilton. Following
lunch, you will come back via the Bacardi
rum plant. After cocktails and dinner, you
will take in one of the many delightful
shows in the area.

SATURDAY

After breakfast, everyone pack your swimming
gear for trip to El Conquistador Hotel. After
lunch, you will be free to go swimming in
either pool or the beach, returning to
San Juan in time for cocktails and dinner.

ST. CROIX
$42.00

TOUR DATES: Jun 18-20, Sep 24-26, Nov 5-7
Three days, two nights $42.00 per person
in double room. Single room $8.00 higher.

FRIDAY
Assemble at Miami Airport one hour prior
to Eastern flight at Counter 35. On arrival
in St. Croix you will be transported to
the ESTATE CARLTON. That evening
Welcome Party by General Manager followed by dinner at hotel.

SATURDAY
Breakfast on the patio, followed by 9 a.m.
departure to Christiansted for boat trip
to Buck Island. Swimming, snorkeling
and a fantastic underwater trail delights
your day. After the boat returns you will
be free to shop in Christiansted. Dinner
that night at the hotel.

SUNDAY
Breakfast at your leisure on the patio.
Time for a last quick dip in the pool or
nine holes of golf at the Estates' own golf
course. Twelve noon departure from
hotel for flight back to Miami.

CONDITIONS

AIR TRANSPORTATION: Passes provided
by Eastern Airlines.

ELIGIBILITY: These tours are available to
all sales personnel in the State of Florida.
This includes reservations, field and city
ticket office agents and their spouse.

HOTELS: First class or deluxe throughout.

MEALS: Meals as listed in each itinerary;
where none listed you are on your own.

TRANSFERS: Included between airport and
hotels.

TOURS: Each itinerary will list the tours
that are included in each package.

TIPS & TAXES: Included for hotels and meals.
Personal items such as room service, valet,
liquor services, extras from regular meal
service and airport taxes are not included.

RESPONSIBILITY: We may alter any of the
itineraries as a result of schedule change
or revised conditions at the destinations.
We reserve the right to adjust the cost or
cancel the tour if the number in the group
is less than that on which arrangements were
predicated.

EASTERN AIRLINES and other transportation companies concerned are not responsible for any act or omission or event during
the time passengers are not on board their
conveyances. The passage contract in use
by the carriers concerned when issued shall
constitute the sole contract between Eastern
Airlines and other transportation companies
and the purchaser of these tours and/or
passenger.

EASTERN

1971
INTERLINE TOURS

EASTERN

NASSAU
$29.00

TOUR DATES: July 21-23, Dec. 1-3.
Three days, two nights $29.00 per person
in double room. Single room higher.

FRIDAY

Check in one hour prior to your Eastern
flight to Nassau. Upon arrival in Nassau
you will be transferred to the FLAGLER
INN on PARADISE ISLAND. Afternoon
free for swim at the Water Bar. Dinner
that evening will be the Merchants Buffet
Dinner and Cocktail Party.

SATURDAY

Breakfast at hotel, then bus will be provided for those who want to sample
Nassau's shopping bargains. Afternoon
is for swimming at the beach or in the
pool. Dinner that evening will be in the
BUCCANEER LOUNGE, following dinner
shuttle to the PARADISE ISLE CASINO
where you may win some money or see
a spectacular revue.

SUNDAY

Breakfast at the Galley Coffee Shop. Manager's Farewell Bloody Mary Party at
11 A.M. Afternoon transfer to airport
for flight back to Miami.
Gratuities not included.

SANTO DOMINGO
$30.00

TOUR DATE: Aug 11-13
Three days, two nights $30.00 per person
in double room. Single room higher.

FRIDAY

Assemble at Eastern's Counter 35 to check
in for Caribair's Flight #953 to Santo
Domingo. After arrival a city tour prior
to check-in at the EMBAJADOR HOTEL.
Cocktails and dinner at the hotel that
night.

SATURDAY

Breakfast early, followed by trip to La
Romana. Lunch at La Romana, afternoon
for swimming, golfing or sunning. Evening
will have a dinner and show.

SUNDAY

Breakfast early again and then transfer to
airport for freeport shopping prior to
boarding flight back to Miami.

SAN JUAN
$39.00

TOUR DATES: Oct 5-8, Nov 16-19
Four days, three nights $39.00 per person
in double room. Single room higher.

THURSDAY

Check in one hour prior to Eastern flight
from Miami. On arrival in San Juan transfer to the DA VINCI HOTEL in the Condado
Suction. Afternoon sightseeing of old San
Juan and the Morro Castle. Evening will
be a welcome cocktail party and dinner at
the hotel.

FRIDAY

Breakfast at hotel, then tour through the
countryside to Dorado where the DORADO
BEACH, the new CERROMAR and the
DORADO HILTON are located. On the re-
turn home stop at the Bacardi Rum plant.
Evening dinner at hotel and evening free to
sample the night life and casinos of San
Juan.

SATURDAY

Breakfast at the hotel, followed by a tour to
El Yunque, the National Rain Forest. Lunch
can be purchased along the way or at the
rain forest. The trip will continue to El
CONQUISTADOR HOTEL, the magnificent
hotel perched on the side of a cliff. That
evening dinner and show at the hotel.

ST. CROIX
$46.00
TOUR DATES: Sept. 22-24, Oct. 20-22.
Three days, two nights $46.00 per person
in double room. Single room $8.00 higher.

FRIDAY
Assemble at Miami Airport one hour prior
to Eastern's flight at Counter 35. On
arrival in St. Croix you will be transported to the Hotel on the Cay. Rest of
afternoon free for shopping or swimming.
Dinner that evening at the Hotel.

SATURDAY
Breakfast on the patio followed by shuttle
to Christiansted for boat trip to Buck
Island. Swimming, snorkeling and a
fantastic underwater trail delights your
day. After the boat returns you will be
free to shop in Christiansted. Dinner that
night at the Hotel.

SUNDAY
Breakfast at your leisure on the patio.
Limited shopping available as most stores
are closed. Time for sunning and swim-
ming before your flight back to Miami.
SERVICE CHARGE IN LIEU OF GRATUI-
TIES INCLUDED.

AIR TRANSPORTATION: Passes provided
by Eastern Airlines.
ELIGIBILITY: These tours are available to
all sales personnel in the State of Florida.
This includes reservations, field and city
ticket office agents and their spouse.
HOTELS: First class or deluxe throughout.
MEALS: Meals as listed in each itinerary;
where none listed you are on your own.
TRANSFERS: Included between airport and
hotels.
TOURS: Each itinerary will list the tours
that are included in each package.
TIPS & TAXES: Included except where noted.
Personal items such as room service, valet,
liquor services, extras from regular meal
service and airport taxes are not included.
RESPONSIBILITY: We may alter any of the
itineraries as a result of schedule change
or revised conditions at the destinations.
We reserve the right to adjust the cost or
cancel the tour if the number in the group is
less than that on which arrangements were
predicated.
EASTERN AIRLINES and other transportation
companies concerned are not responsible for
any act or omission or event during the time
passengers are not on board their conveyances. The passage contract in use by the
carriers concerned when issued shall constitute the sole contract between Eastern Airlines and other transportation companies and
the purchaser of these tours and/or passenger.

EASTERN

74-PP-0787   9/70   150M   Printed in U.S.A.

INTERLINE TOURS
1972

NASSAU
$29.00

TOUR DATES: July 21-23, Dec. 1-3.
Three days, two nights $29.00 per person
in double room. Single room higher.
FRIDAY
Check in one hour prior to your Eastern
flight to Nassau. Upon arrival in Nassau
you will be transferred to the FLAGLER
INN on PARADISE ISLAND. Afternoon
free for swim at the Water Bar. Dinner
that evening will be the Merchants Buffet
Dinner and Cocktail Party.
SATURDAY
Breakfast at hotel, then bus will be provided for those who want to sample
Nassau's shopping bargains. Afternoon
is for swimming at the beach or in the
pool. Dinner that evening will be in the
BUCCANEER LOUNGE, following dinner
shuttle to the PARADISE ISLE CASINO
where you may win some money or see
a spectacular revue.
SUNDAY
Breakfast at the Galley Coffee Shop. Manager's Farewell Bloody Mary Party at
11 A.M. Afternoon transfer to airport
for flight back to Miami.
Gratuities not included.

SANTO DOMINGO
$30.00

TOUR DATE: Aug 11-13
Three days, two nights $30.00 per person
in double room. Single room higher.
FRIDAY
Assemble at Eastern's Counter 35 to check
in for Caribair's Flight #953 to Santo
Domingo. After arrival a city tour prior
to check-in at the EMBAJADOR HOTEL.
Cocktails and dinner at the hotel that
night.
SATURDAY
Breakfast early, followed by trip to La
Romana. Lunch at La Romana, afternoon
for swimming, golfing or running. Evening
will have a dinner and show.
SUNDAY
Breakfast early again and then transfer to
airport for freeport shopping prior to
boarding flight back to Miami.

SAN JUAN
$39.00

TOUR DATES: Oct 5-8, Nov 16-19
Four days, three nights $39.00 per person
in double room. Single room higher.
THURSDAY
Check in one hour prior to Eastern flight
from Miami. On arrival in San Juan trans-
fer to the DA VINCI HOTEL in the Condado
Section. Afternoon sightseeing of old San
Juan and the Morro Castle. Evening will
be a welcome cocktail party and dinner at
the hotel.
FRIDAY
Breakfast at hotel, then tour through the
countryside to Dorado where the DORADO
BEACH, the new CERROMAR and the
DORADO HILTON are located. On the return home stop at the Bacardi Rum plant.
Evening dinner at hotel and evening free to
sample the night life and casinos of San
Juan.
SATURDAY
Breakfast at the hotel, followed by a tour to
El Yunque, the National Rain Forest. Lunch
can be purchased along the way or at the
rain forest. The trip will continue to EL
CONQUISTADOR HOTEL, the magnificent
hotel perched on the side of a cliff. That
evening dinner and show at the hotel.

MARTINIQUE
$65.00

TOUR DATES: October 25-28, 1974
Four days, three nights $65.00 per person in double room. Single rooms higher.

FRIDAY
Check in one hour prior to Eastern flight from Miami. Flight 953 will depart at 1:30 pm. On arrival in Martinique you will be transferred to the MARTINIQUE HILTON. Dinner that evening will be at the hotel.

SATURDAY
Breakfast at leisure. The day will be free to visit Fort de France, the capital city and search for shopping bargains or time to enjoy the sun and beach. Dinner that night at hotel.

SUNDAY
Breakfast at hotel, then get ready for a tour around Martinique, one of the most mountainous islands in the Caribbean, home of Mt. Pelee, an active volcano. Dinner again at the hotel.

MONDAY
Breakfast at the hotel and depart for the airport for the trip home.

IDENTIFICATION MUST BE CARRIED SUCH AS A PASSPORT OR VOTER REGISTRATION. DRIVER'S LICENSE IS NOT SUFFICIENT.

CONDITIONS

AIR TRANSPORTATION: Passes provided by Eastern Airlines.

ELIGIBILITY: These tours are available to all sales personnel in the State of Florida. This includes reservations, field and city ticket office agents and their spouse.

HOTELS: First class or deluxe throughout.

MEALS: Meals as listed in each itinerary; where none listed you are on your own.

TRANSFERS: Included between airport and hotels.

TOURS: Each itinerary will list the tours that are included in each package.

TIPS & TAXES: Included for hotels and meals. Personal items such as room service, valet, liquor services, extras from regular meal service and airport taxes are not included.

RESPONSIBILITY: We may alter any of the itineraries as a result of schedule change or revised conditions at the destinations. We reserve the right to adjust the cost or cancel the tour if the number in the group is less than that on which arrangements were predicated.

EASTERN AIRLINES and other transportation companies concerned are not responsible for any act or omission or event during the time passengers are not on board their conveyances. The passage contract in use by the carriers concerned when issued shall constitute the sole contract between Eastern Airlines and other transportation companies and the purchaser of these tours and/or passenger.

EASTERN

INTERLINE TOURS
1974

MEXICO CITY
$79.00
TOUR DATES: September 12-15, 1974
Four days, three nights $79.00 per person
in double room. Single room higher.

THURSDAY
Check in one hour prior to Eastern flight
from Miami. Flight 907 will depart at 9 am.
On arrival in Mexico City transfer to the
MARIA ISABEL SHERATON. Afternoon city
tour of Mexico City. Dinner that night at
DELMONICO's famous restaurant.

FRIDAY
All day tour to TAXCO and CUERNAVACA
with lunch in TAXCO.

SATURDAY
Tour to the archaeological zone and the
pyramids of TEOTIHUACAN. Afternoon free
for shopping. Dinner that night at DEL LAGO
a most beautiful restaurant in Chapultepec
Park.

SUNDAY
Morning free for trip to the Museum or the
Folklore Ballet. Checkout at 12 noon for re-
turn to Miami.

Be sure to obtain MEXICAN TOURIST CARD
BEFORE reaching the airport.

ARUBA
$65.00
TOUR DATES: November 7-10, 1974
Four days, three nights $65.00 per person
in double room. Single room higher.

THURSDAY
Check in one hour prior to Eastern flight
from Miami. Flight 953 will depart 1:30 pm.
On arrival in Aruba you will be transferred
to the ARUBA HOLIDAY INN.

FRIDAY
Breakfast at the hotel, then tour around the
island. Dinner that night will be at the
hotel.

SATURDAY
Breakfast at your leisure. The day will be
free for freeport shopping or swimming on
some of the most beautiful beaches in the
world. Dinner will again be at the hotel.

SUNDAY
Breakfast at the hotel and then depart the
hotel for return trip to Miami.

BARBADOS
$65.00
TOUR DATES: September 26-29, 1974
Four days, three nights $65.00 per person
in double room. Single rooms higher.

THURSDAY
Check in one hour prior to Eastern flight
from Miami. On arrival in Barbados you will be transferred to the BARBADOS HILTON. Dinner
that evening will be at the hotel.

FRIDAY
Breakfast at the hotel, then tour around the
island of Barbados, one of the most English
islands. Dinner that evening will again be
at the hotel.

SATURDAY
Breakfast at your leisure. The rest of the
day will be free for shopping in Bridgetown
the capital city of Barbados, or swimming
at the beautiful beach at the hotel. Dinner
at the hotel.

SUNDAY
Breakfast at the hotel and depart the hotel
for return trip to Miami.

ARUBA

Eastern Airlines & Sheraton Hotels
June 21, 22, 23, 24, 1973

Stay at Sheraton Aruba 3 nights
Transfers to and from Hotel-Airport
3 Breakfasts, 3 Lunches, 3 Dinners

THUR JUN 21   Depart MIA 0730 Arrive Aruba 3^{35}pm
               Dinner at Sheraton Aruba

FRI JUN 22   Breakfast at Sheraton
               Tour of Island by De Palms Tours
               Lunch at *Divi Divi* Hotel
               Dinner at Holiday Inn

SAT JUN 23   Breakfast at Sheraton
               Lunch at Aruba Caribbean Hotel
               Dinner at the Coral Strand Hotel

SUN JUN 24   Breakfast at Sheraton
               Lunch at Manchebo Hotel

               Depart Aruba 4^{00}pm Arrive Miami 10^{45}pm

Price 32^{00}

Call Larry Green 873-2717

160

ANTIGUA

EASTERN AIRLINES
AUGUST 25, 26, 27, 28, 1973

STAY AT THE INN
3 NIGHTS, TRANSFERS TO
AND FROM HOTEL
3 BREAKFASTS - 2 DINNERS
SIGHTSEEING TOUR OF ISLAND

SAT AUG 25
DEPART MIAMI 4^{15} PM ARRIVE ANTIGUA 9^{08} PM

TUES AUG 28
DEPART ANTIGUA 10^{45} PM ARRIVE MIAMI 4^{26} PM

PRICE $52^{00}

CALL LARRY GREEN 873-2717

◢ EASTERN

BARBADOS

BARBADOS HILTON

4 DAYS - 3 NIGHTS   MAY 1-4, 1975
3 BREAKFASTS - 3 DINNERS
TRANSFERS TO AND FROM AIRPORT
RUM COCKTAIL PARTY
AFTERNOON CRUISE

$70.00

AIRLINE SALES PERSONNEL ONLY, FIRST COME
FIRST CONFIRMED. CALL LARRY GREEN 873-2717
SEND LETTER OF EMPLOYMENT AND CHECK TO LARRY
AT 700 FIRST NATIONAL BANK BUILDING

EASTERN

Puerto Rico   Sheraton

4 DAYS - 3 NIGHTS   JUNE 26-29, 1975
3 BREAKFASTS - 3 DINNERS
TRANSFERS TO AND FROM AIRPORT
COCKTAIL PARTY
TOUR OF CITY AND COUNTRYSIDE

$55.00

AIRLINE SALES PERSONNEL FIRST COME
FIRST CONFIRMED. CALL LARRY GREEN 873-2717
SEND LETTER OF EMPLOYMENT AND CHECK TO LARRY
AT 700 FIRST NATIONAL BANK BUILDING

DEPART MIAMI #951 AT 2$\frac{00}{PM}$ RETURN 964 AT 3$\frac{50}{PM}$

163

EASTERN

Maria Isabel-   **Sheraton Hotel**

4 DAYS - 3 NIGHTS   SEPTEMBER 27-30, 1975

TRANSFERS TO AND FROM AIRPORT

HALF DAY TOUR OF CITY

FULL DAY TOUR TO TAXCO AND CUERNAVACA

TWO DINNERS — ONE LUNCH

$75⁰⁰

AIRLINE SALES PERSONNEL — FIRST COME

FIRST CONFIRMED. CALL LARRY GREEN 873-271

SEND LETTER OF EMPLOYMENT AND CHECK TO LARRY

AT 700 FIRST NATIONAL BANK BUILDING

DEPART MIAMI #907 AT 8:15 — RETURN #906 — 9:5

164

EASTERN

st. maarten

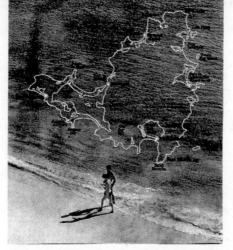

4 DAYS - 3 NIGHTS   OCTOBER 8-11, 1976

3 BREAKFASTS   3 DINNERS

TRANSFERS TO AND FROM AIRPORT

TOUR OF THE ISLAND

$55 00

AIRLINE SALES PERSONNEL   FIRST COME
FIRST CONFIRMED. CALL LARRY GREEN 873-2717
SEND LETTER OF EMPLOYMENT AND CHECK TO
LARRY AT 4890 NW 36TH STREET 33148
DEPART MIAMI ON #915 AT 9 20 AM RETURN #966 AT 8 12 PM

165

MEXICO

EASTERN AIRLINES
 SEPTEMBER 18, 19, 20, 21, 22, 1975

STAY AT FIESTA PALACE HOTEL
 5 DAYS 4 NIGHTS
 TRANSFERS TO AND FROM HOTEL
 WELCOME COCKTAIL PARTY
 TOUR OF MEXICO CITY
 TOUR TO PYRAMIDS
 TOUR TO TAXCO

I BREAKFAST, 3 LUNCHES, I DINNER

SEPT 18 DEPART MIAMI 7:00 AM
SEPT 22 ARRIVE MIAMI 9:35 PM
 PRICE $59.00

CALL LARRY GREEN 873-2717

interoffice correspondence   ◣ EASTERN

TO: Mr. L. C. Green   ADDRESS: MIASP

FROM: D. F. Noonan   ADDRESS: MIASP

SUBJECT: Congratulations   DATE: Jan. 28, 1975

Larry, just a personal note of congratulations concerning your selection as "Interline Man Of The Year."

I was very pleased when I learned of this outstanding recognition given by your peers and I can think of no one more deserving of this honor than you.

Keep up the good work.

D. F. Noonan

cc: Mr. Bill Gregg

With the deregulation the airlines could pay the agents any commission they wanted. We had strong suspicions that some airlines had been paying big accounts under the table for years and now we could compete with them out in the open. Eastern decided to pay incentives to those agencies that could move business to Eastern. For the first few years the sales managers handled all the incentive schemes. Then the executive office decided to handle it from there and transferred in accountants and other people with no knowledge of sales or the territories they were handling. In my opinion a very bad decision. For example when I was handling the incentives for Miami I had a new travel agent come to me to ask for incentive pay. I turned him down as he had no track record. The man returned asking again and said he could make any amount I needed to give him an incentive. I said alright you give us $50,000.00 a month and we will give you 1% and scale it up from there. He made the $50,000.00 to $60,000.00 every month. Under the new system he would not have even gotten to talk to anyone and Eastern would have lost $50,000.00 to $60,000.00 a month.

In April 1973 Eastern took over the routes of Caribair in the Caribbean. The Home Office was going to set up familiarization trips for Eastern sales personnel and the travel agents. The system agency manager was Paul -----(I can't remember) and he was going to use Caribbean Holidays for the ground arrangements. At the last minute the head of Caribbean Holidays took off and the company went bankrupt. Recently someone who worked for Caribbean Holiday said it was the bookkeeper who took all the money. Anyway Paul called me and asked if I could set up these trips to the Caribbean, using my information from the trips I ran and my familiarity with the area. I said I could if he let me use the wholesaler I wanted. He said yes. I had worked with Ruth (Colson) Magnet when she was with GoGo and then with Flyfaire and I wanted to use her as I

168

could trust her to do things right. I ended up scheduling all the trips from about every city into the Caribbean, picking the city with the best connection to an island for their trip. This got Flyfaire into to the Caribbean big time and in with Eastern. Not that I expected anything but I didn't even get a thank you from Joe Garzilli, but it all worked out well. Eastern then became the dominant force in the Caribbean but at least we were not out to kill the small regional airlines such as happens today. We has a live and let live attitude.

My boss from about 1972, Don Noonan, was the District Sales Manager then the Regional Sales Manager and he used to say to me "the problem with you is you don't blow your own horn enough". Well I didn't, the fact that I was doing something positive for Eastern Airlines was what I cared about. It sounds self effusive but it was true. Now I am making a little toot.

Don and I got along well together. I continued to do a lot of the work I did as Regional Sales Administrator. I did all the budgets and worked out all the salary increases after I got Don's feeling about each sales rep. I also worked out most of the sales promotion schemes.

One of the first programs was to get a piece of the Mexico business from Miami. We had a flight that when from Miami to New Orleans to Mexico. It left early in the morning and the return from Mexico City was in the afternoon. The competitive nonstop flights all left in the afternoon and returned in the morning. I felt this gave us an advantage of more time in Mexico and more covenant times for both the business traveler and the leisure traveler.

The best fares were for group travel called FITs, which were a package of airline and ground arrangements. I called Mexico Travel Advisors and worked out FITs with them. The problem was you had to have 15 people to make the trip go. We were not doing to well on this then I found out from a travel agent friend that when he went to book Eastern he was advised Eastern would probably not get the 15 people so the group would be canceled he would be better booking on the competition as their groups went. I checked this out and found they did go but they counted by twos as each person went out the door. (In other words they did not have the 15 either but sent the group anyway).

Don complained to Frank Sharpe but was told we had to catch them at it in order to make the charge stick. Well we were not going to go to the airport and check their tickets so I dropped the program and waited my time.

I called Ruth Magnet and asked her when Flyfaire was going to go into Mexico City. She said she thought it would be soon. In the mean time there was a change in the tariff that said if the airline had a group of 15 people and anyone canceled at the last minute the group could still go. That was my chance, after that we ALWAYS had 15 people but unfortunately three or four canceled at the last minute. When Flyfaire started operating in Mexico City Ruth and I had a big promotion for the travel agents. We held it at the Holiday Inn at 22nd Street on Miami Beach. We got Wilburt Sanchez of the Mexico Travel Bureau and Marichies (southwest 8th street mariachies), Ruth and I were the frick and frack on the sales features.

The flight worked out very well and Don asked me how I got it going and I said you really don't want to know (meaning 15 people who *traveled*) and Don said OK (he was a pretty straight guy). Later in the year we had a company sales meeting at Walt Disney World. The Summer schedule had come out and we lost the flight to Mexico. I caught Mort Ehrlich, who was Vice President and in charge of schedules, between sessions and asked him why the Mexico flight was canceled. Mort said right away he was sorry but they had not checked how well the flight was doing recently and they would put it back on the Fall schedule.

By CHUCK REITENBACH And LARRY CAFIERO

ADM. RICHARD POOR, USN RET. is the new president of the Greater Miami Aviation Association. Also elected were first vice president. Tack Marshall, EAL captain; second vice president. Robert Diaz, ground operation, MIA, USAF Col. Ret.; third vice president. Walter Robshaw, National Airlines; treasurer. Dan Sifford, chairman, Overseas Aviation Corp.; and secretary, Gil Smith, president Overseas Aviation Corp. Admiral Pool succeeded Jim Frazier, former FAA executive.

THE TRAVEL INDUSTRY'S NEW fric and frac, Larry Green, Eastern Airlines, and Ruth Magnet, Flyfaire of Miami, did their number outlining new offerings to Mexico, along with Mexican National Tourist Council Miami chief Wilbert Sanchez. Wilbert, in fact, made two speeches within 13 hours at the Sheraton River House. One at the Flyfaire-Eastern presentation, then at Mexicana's breakfast. Reminder: there are 22 pesos to the dollar.

TRAVEL INDUSTRY ASSOCIATION OF FLORIDA presenting seminar on "The Successful Selling of Travel" at Omni May 3, 8:30 a.m. to 5 p.m. Subjects include telephone sales techniques; selling up; cruises; car rentals; increasing group and incentive sales; legal liability of the travel agent; and a panel discussion. Price is $10 including luncheon. For more details, call Ruth Feigenbaum, Kendall Travel. Next TIA meeting is April 20. Casa Santino Restaurant. 6:30 p.m. Speaker is Dr. Emilio Tommasi, travel commissioner for the Italian Government Travel Office. Topic, "Italy on Sale," stresses value of U.S. dollar in Italy.

This is the travel column from the Miami Herald commenting on the Mexico program. They did not mention our "Eighth Street Mariachis" who were great leading off the promotion.

Later we got a nonstop flight to Mexico City when Pan Am gave up their Miami-Mexico City route saying they couldn't make any money on it. We took it over and made money on the flight, then 6 or 8 months later they wanted the route back and they got it..

Don Noonan dreamed up a very nice program that became a yearly outing and that was a golf day with Chi Chi Rodriguez. Don found out Chi Chi was on retainer with Eastern Airlines and he would come and play golf with us for a day. Chi Chi was also the pro at the Dorado Beach Hotel, which Eastern owned. Don invited all the commercial accounts and freight forwarders and had me get all the agents that played golf.

Don set up the day at Doral Country Club for the first three years, then went to Aventura Country Club for one year, then back to the Doral for another year or so. We would pair up the foursomes, Chi Chi would put on a golf demonstration with some very neat shots, then we would play a shotgun tournament after which we would have a buffet reception. Chi Chi would talk and tell a few jokes (he was funny). Chi Chi was a very nice man, humble, patriotic and caring. He funded a children's program in Tampa for years. It was a great day and all our customers appreciated it (and gave us more business).The agents looked forward to playing each year.

November 11, 1980

Dear Travel Agent and/or
Golfers, Hackers and Duffers:

Eastern Airlines has corralled the services of
one of the top golfers, Chi Chi Rodriguez, who has
consented to spend a day with the travel people of
Miami.

Chi Chi will give a demonstration on December 2nd
at 11:00am at the Doral Country Club. We will then
have a golfing day where Chi Chi will play one hole
with each team of four. We will have a shotgun start
(that's where every team starts on a different hole),
and an awards (?) party after the game.

Any travel agent who has a set of clubs is welcome
to play (men, women, etc.), handicaps are of no con-
sequence (my handicap is the clubs). Join us, it will
be a fun day. R.S.V.P. to 873-2717.

Sincerely,

Lawrence C. Green, CTC
Manager Agency Sales

LCG:en

Golf Day with Chi Chi Rodriguez, 1979 at Aventura? Don Noonan, Chi Chi, Larry

Wally Bithorn, Larry, Chi Chi, Ruby Levine, Art Horwitz

As sales manager I set up a travel agency advisory council. We would meet for dinner and discuss the current problems between the agencies and the airlines. We had six members on the council but I don't remember all the names. I know we had Joe Vendi, Marilyn Holland (Mansanilla), Jim Eraso, Gene Stevens and Barbara Weinkle and I think Ann Chesney. Marilyn had been to an ICTA (Institute of Certified Travel Agents) meeting and brought to the table the idea that agents all over the country thought Florida agents were nothing but Mom and Pop agencies - not professionals. We all disagreed with this assessment and what came out of that was the first ICTA classes in Miami. I said I would start the classes if Marilyn would be our coordinator/professor. Marilyn agreed and I sent out a flyer to all agencies advising the time and place for the formation of the class.

We were fortunate that EASTERN had a great training facility on the base on NW 36th Street called the Hartley building. It was named for an Eastern pilot who was hijacked and shot but got the plane and all the passengers down safely. Now Dade County has taken over the building and has taken the name off which is a shame. The building was used to train pilots in the classrooms and the flight simulators in the building. I got the use of one of the classrooms for Mondays nights.

The formation meeting had 28 attendees. Of these 22 people worked though the next year and a half, taking four tests on management and agency functions. The test were all taken at newly started FIU in the Prima Casa building with a strict monitor supervising the class and the time. This all cumulated in the degree of CTC (Certified Travel Consultant) at the University of Colorado in 1976. (See picture)Up to that time Dade county had only one agent who worked for his CTC and that was Ernie Lara of Travelwise. We had four or five agents grandfathered in as CTC because of their long time and experience as travel agents. After a few years I took over as coordinator/professor for about ten years before I got tired an quit. That was pretty much the end of organized ICTA training in Miami.

ICTA started destination specialist programs for travel agents some time after that and a group of us got together to take the Caribbean Specialist program. We even got Larry Cafiero (a travel writer, first with the Miami Herald then his own paper the Southeast Travel Pro), to take the course with us. It was about a three month course followed by a strictly monitored test. All but three past the test. I am really a Caribbean specialist having visited most of the islands. I counted up recently and found I had stayed in 102 different hotels in the Caribbean (including the Bahamas) and some of them three or four times. Many countries after that started specialist programs on their country and even some of the hotels did the same thing. The Bahamas started their own program and I was certified as a Bahamas Expert with group of others. (See picture).

Top row: Jerry Cusmanno, Lucette Prestegaard, Ann Chesney, Pearl Nina, Carlos DeGabriel, Larry Green, Joe Vendi
Bottom: John Siefkes, Bill Cooper, Edward Fogarty, Dr. Edward Kelly, Art Horwitz, Harriet Horwitz, Marilyn Holland, Barbara Weinkle, Zelda Rosenthal, Allen Norlem, Ed Wohlmuth. Picture taken at the Univ of Colorado 1976

BAHAMAS BRIEFING

Vol. 2 No. 1
                                        Winter, 1987

Bahamas Experts Receive Plaques

Plaques were recently awarded to participants in Bahamas Expert Seminars throughout Florida on behalf of the Deputy Prime Minister, Minister of Tourism and Minister of Foreign Affairs for The Bahamas, the Honourable Clement T. Maynard.

Receiving plaques were travel agents, tour operators and airline representatives who participated in on-shore educational seminars held in Freeport in May and Nassau in June, 1986. The seminars were sponsored by the Bahamas Ministry of Tourism and The Bahamas Hotel Association.

Due to the overwhelming, favourable response from participants, a series of Bahamas Expert Seminars is planned for Spring, 1987. They will take the form of half-day seminars in cities throughout Florida, followed by special on-shore familiarization trips to the Family Islands, Nassau/Cable Beach/Paradise Island and Freeport, Grand Bahama. Plaques will only be given to participants in the half-day seminar and the on-shore familiarization trip.

We cordially invite you to become a Bahamas Expert. If you would like to participate or nominate a colleague to participate, please fill out the application in this newsletter and return it to the Bahamas Tourist Office, 255 Alhambra Circle, Suite 425, Coral Gables, Florida 33134. A schedule of seminars and the curriculum are listed for your convenience.

The Bahamas Tourist Office shows here a Tourist Office staffer, Lindie Merritt, Larry Green, A Tourist Officer staffer, Betty Gore, Tyrone Sawyer Director of the Tourist Office, Tracey Mulhousen and Woody Wilson of the Tourist Office. The three ladies were members of the A Team who assisted the Eastern sales office.

In 1975 the Caribbean Tourism Organization wanted to start a chapter in Miami and had a formation meeting at the Ramada Hotel. I helped form the chapter and was on the original board of directors. I have been on the board ever since. Eastern was the biggest airline into the Caribbean and I felt we needed to be in the organization. I was elected president for the years of 1986 and 1987. Naturally we took the members to places like Haiti, Dominican Republic, the Bahamas and St Thomas. I was president again from mid 1992 thru December 1994 rebuilding the organization from about 23 members (after hurricane Andrew) back to160 members.

We had a real nice incentive for the travel agents. Joe Lynch, who was agency specialist in the home office, had gotten money for agency plaques to award those agencies who achieved the greatest percent increase year over year. Once a year we gave out plaques to the Miami travel agents in a special lunch at the Marriott in flight kitchen near the airport. Mr. Adolpho Minoso was the manager and he had a fine dinning room on the second floor. Adolpho would have the waiters take the first class meals right off the production line and serve them to the agents complete with EASTERN chinaware, utensils, glassware and wine. It was a great lunch and an award the agents looked forward to achieve. (See picture)

I started another program which I think helped the very strong rapport that EASTERN had with the travel agents. I had three sales representatives calling on agents in Dade County. I had two reps each month select one their agencies who did an outstanding job for EASTERN. The rep would invite the agency for dinner at any restaurant of their choice. (I had to cross out four or five restaurants that were too expensive). We had to limit the number from the really big agencies but got to talk to many the front line workers. It was also nice duty for me as I got to go once or twice a month for a nice dinner. This built a lot of good will that translated into many sales for Eastern. And the agents could vent any problems with the company on me. Today they can't even find a sales manager. We usually had Gloria Golden or a res agent at the dinner and that helped also, our gals were just great and they did a wonderful job with the travel agents.

This is one of our dinners where the sales rep entertained one of their best producers. It this case these are the people from Carnival Cruise Lines air /sea desk. The second person from the left is Cheryl Parker who was a superb sale representative for Eastern.

This was one of the dinners at Food Among The Flowers. The people are from the Carnival Air/Sea Desk. The second person on the left is Cheryl Parker, one of our best sales reps. This was one of her accounts.

In the Fall of 1975 Bill Gregg wanted to move the sales office from downtown to the airport area and the reservations building had some space for us. We had some objections among then the parking. Bill was very nice to us because he could have said you are going and that's it. He promised Don and I our own parking places and let me design the area for the office. I drew up the plans which gave Don Noonan, Lou Greenwell, Luis Palacio and myself a private office.

The first door to the office had Marie Cowart, who was now Don Noonan's secretary, up front and Nedra Swasey, who was my secretary, behind her. On the left side was Luis's office and then mine. On the right was the large office for Don. The second door was to the sales reps area and their secretary and behind that Lou's office.

It worked out well because across the hall from us was the executive desk with Gloria Golden, Bernie Paro and all the executive desk agents. We now had access to the people who could help us with reservations problems. I can't tell you how much help all these people were to Eastern and to me. I learned how to use the reservation computer from them and had my own pass code to get in. I could check the flights and see what condition they were in.

For years the district sales manager held space on some heavily booked flights in the peak periods. The reservations manager, I believe it was Ed McCrystal, came to me ans asked if they could take the seats back and reservations would guarantee to get any seats we needed. He explained it would be much more efficient way to manage the seats. I agreed and I understood that once in a while when a flight was sold out- it was sold out. When I needed a seat I would ask Gloria or Bernie Paro for it and would get it in a short time. Sometimes Gloria said "there is no way" for a certain flight and I would tell who ever wanted the seat to pick another flight as that one was NOT going to clear.

As I said our executive desk agents were wonderful. They loved Eastern Airlines and their work and it showed. They were very helpful to our travel agents and the commercial accounts. If they were asked for a seat on a certain flight and it was sold out, they would take a post-it note and write it down and stick it on the computer. Then they would check all day (if they liked you) to see if a seat opened up and they got many seats that way. Another way they got seats was to notify the agents around them what flight they needed. When an agent got a cancellation for that flight that agent would set up the cancellation to the point of the enter key, then the first agent, that needed the seat, would set up the sell function, the agent cancelling would hit the enter key and the other agent would count about 5 or 6 seconds and hit the enter key on her computer and probably got the seat. I could only remember a few of the names of our great executive team so I called Bernie Paro and he gave me some more. If I leave any of them out blame Bernie. We had Lenore Bachman, Mina Benedetto, Hazel Bergstrom, Van (Vanessa) Camp, Gloria Chapman, Lorraine McCarthy, Mia McKay, Esther Mather, Hazel Nierenberg, Kattie Pendling, Flo Penny and Gene Robinson. Thanks Ladies.

When Chuck Wilcoxen was sales manager I did a passenger forecast for him and he sent it in. When that season ended there was a whoha about why Miami was right on the forecast and the home office was off. Anyway when Don Noonan came in I did a forecast on every big schedule change. We had over 100 flights to account for. The forecast were for three or four months. I would go over every flight by month and forecast my numbers for each flight. I used last years figures, new competition, state of the economy, trends in tourist destinations, (I read Travel Weekly and Travel Agent magazine which gave me a lot of information) and used what ever knowledge I had of the industry as a whole. I was one of the few who were permitted to discuss the forecasts with the forecasters in the home office, first Cy Cardillo and then Jim Sheehan. I would take my figures in and we would go over every flight and discuss why we came up with the numbers we had. It was amazing some times we hit the number right on the head and we were never far off on any of them.

In 1976 thru 1978 we had Lucette Prestegard, who was president of "Your Travel Agent", and Allen Norlem, who was vice president, arrange a number of trips with British Airways to take European travel agents from Europe to visit the United States. Lucette was born in Switzerland and spoke many languages and Allen was born in Denmark also spoke a number of languages.

JANUARY 10 BRITISH AIRWAYS GROUP FROM FINLAND
TOUR MANAGER: LEHTOVIRTA, MR. K., BRITISH AIRWAYS,
HELSINKI.   1976

NAME	AFFILIATION	TITLE
2. Groundstroem, Mrs. E.	Area Travel, Helsinki	Sen. Office Mgr.
3. Hacklin, Mrs. A.	Finland S/S Co., Helsinki	Asst. Sales Mgr.
4. Kangrvo, Mrs. L.	Kaleva Travel Jyvaskyla	Travel Agent
5. Konni, Mrs. L.	Kaleva Travel, Helsinki	Sen. Travel Agt.
6. Koski, Mrs. M.	Porin Matkatoimisto, Pori	Sen. Travel Agt.
7. Lundell, Mrs. R.	Finland Travel Bureau, Seinajoki	Travel Agent
8. Manninen, Mr. H.	Finland Travel Bureau, Helsinki	Asst. Sales Mgr.
9. Mantere, Miss R.	United Travel, Helsinki	Travel Agt., USA Dept.
10. Osterman, Mrs. S.	Travek Travel Bureau, Helsinki	Dept. Manager
11. Rasanen, Mrs. T.	Airtours Helsinki, Helsinki	Sen. Travel Agt.

Total: 11 participants and local tour escort, Mr. Allan Norlem.

EA 792   JAN 14   MIA/MCO

EA 861   JAN 16   MCO/MIA

AIRPORT COMPUTER FAC. VISIT

LOUNGE AVAIL. FOR HAND BAGG. + DRINK 5⁰⁰

187

YOUR TRAVEL AGENT, INC.
LUCETTE PRESTEGAARD, PRESIDENT
386 MIRACLE MILE, CORAL GABLES, FLORIDA 33134
TEL. (305) 446-8232

JANUARY 24-28, 1976

FAMILIARIZATION TRIP, ITINERARY B

BRITISH AIRWAYS TRAVEL AGENTS GROUP FROM THE

MIDDLE EAST.

PARTICIPANTS:	AFFILIATION:	TITLE:
1. WHINCOP, Mr. Phillip	British Airways, Tehran	District Sales Mgr. & (Tour Manager)
2. AFTANDILAIAN, Mr. V.	Transair Travel, Tehran	Finance Director.
3. BOUDAKUH, Mr. Y.	Service Tours Travel, Tehran	Director.
4. DAVOUDIAN, Mr. J.	Universal Travel, Tehran	Reservation Mgr.
5. HIKAZ, Mr.	Persepoulis Travel, Tehran	Director of Sales.
6. KYLING, Mr. J.	Persian Gulf Travel Agency, Tehran	Director.
7. MINASIAN, Mr. A.	Phoenicia Travel, Tehran	Travel Manager.
8. MOHAJERI, Mr. M.	Mohajeri Tours, Tehran	Director.
9. SANAI, Mr. S.	Irtuc Travel, Tehran	Sales Manager.
10. SHARIFI, Mr. H.	Monvoyages, Tehran	Director.
11. SMITH, Mr. G.	Thos. Cook, Baghdad, Iraq	Manager.

LOCAL TOUR ESCORTS::Mrs. Lucette J. Prestegaard and/or
Mr. Allan Norlem.

188

YOUR TRAVEL AGENT, INC.
LUCETTE PRESTEGAARD, PRESIDENT
386 MIRACLE MILE, CORAL GABLES, FLORIDA 33134
TEL. (305) 446-8232

FEBRUARY 7 - 11, 1976
FAMILIARIZATION TRIP, ITINERARY B
BRITISH AIRWAYS TRAVEL AGENTS GROUP FROM SAUDI ARABIA,
BAHRAIN, UNITED ARAB EMIRATES, AND OMAN.

PARTICIPANTS:	AFFILIATION:	TITLE:
1. MR. JOHN CHACKO	British Airways, Bahrain	Senior Sales Rep.
2. MR. EUGENE GILLESPIE	International Agency, Dhahran	Asst. Mgr.
3. MR. JUDE GONSALVES	Gray Mackenzie, Abu Dhabi	Supervisor.
4. MR. ABDUL RAHMAN JAAFAR	Gray Mackenzie, Travel, Bahrain	Mgr.
5. MR. JOE KHOURY	Jet Travel, Dhahran	Mgr.
6. MR. DAVID MORRIS	Kanoo Travel Agency, Bahrain	Mgr.
7. MR. FARIZ NAKKASH	Algaith Travel Agency, Abu Dhabi	Mgr.
8. MR. ASAD RAZA	Zubair Travel and Service Bureau, Muscat	Mgr.
9. MR. SASEEDARAN	Omeir Travel Agency, Abu Dhabi	Reservations Officer.
10. MR. MANOHAR TARABAGIL	Kanoo Travel Agency, Alkhobar	Mgr.
11. MR. PIERRE ZEEWARDER	International Travel Bureau, Bahrain	Mgr.

LOCAL TOUR ESCORTS: Mrs. Lucette J. Prestegaard or Mr. Allan Norlem.

YOUR TRAVEL AGENT, INC.
LUCETTE PRESTEGAARD, PRESIDENT
366 MIRACLE MILE, CORAL GABLES, FLORIDA 33134
TEL. (305) 446-6232

FEBRUARY 28 - MARCH 5, 1976

FAMILIARIZATION TRIP, ITINERARY A

BRITISH AIRWAYS TRAVEL AGENTS GROUP FROM

IRELAND.

PARTICIPANTS:	AFFILIATION:	TITLE:
1. Mr. Bernard WARD	British Airways, Dublin	Sr. Sales Rep. TOUR LEADER
2. Mr. Tony BRAZIL	Limerick Travel, Limerick	Director
3. Mr. J. BRASSIL	Four Seasons Travel, Navan	Owner
4. Mr. B. CASEY	B. Casey Travel, Cork	Owner
5. Mr. J. HASTINS	Heffernan's Travel, Cork	Manager
6. Mr. J. LOFTUS	Intercontinental Travel, Dublin	Owner
7. Mr. S. McLOUGHNEY	Twohigs Travel, Dublin	Business/Travel Mgr.
8. Mr. J. ODONOGHUE	Swann / Ryan Travel, Dublin	Manager
9. Mr. N. PHELAN	Lep Travel, Dublin	Manager
10. Mr. Martin RYAN	Martins Travel, Dublin	Owner
11. Mr. Patrick SCOTT	Scotts Travel, Arklow	Owner
12. Mr. Francis TULLY	Tully Travel, Carlow	Owner

12 PARTICIPANTS

Local Tour Escort: Mrs. Lucette J. Prestegaard or
                      Mr. Allan Norlem.

YOUR TRAVEL AGENT, INC.
LUCETTE PRESTEGAARD, PRESIDENT
396 MIRACLE MILE, CORAL GABLES, FLORIDA 33134
TEL. (305) 446-8232

MARCH 13 - 19, 1976

BRITISH AIRWAYS TRAVEL AGENTS GROUP

FROM

SWITZERLAND

PARTICIPANTS	AFFILIATION	TITLE
1. Mr. W. HIESTAND	BRITISH AIRWAYS, Zurich	Sen. Sales Repres. (Tour Manager)
2. Mr. R. BAUMANN	DANZAS TRAVEL, Biel	Branch Manager
3. Mr. J. BRANCH	KUONI TRAVEL, Interlaken	Manager
4. Mr. G. BRUNNER	THOS. COOK, UNO, Geneve	Assist. Manager
5. Mr. A. CACHIN	VERON GRAUER, Geneve	Travel Agent
6. Mrs. D. GIRARDET	AVY VOYAGES, Yverdon	Travel Agent
7. Mr. W. MAURER	FERT TRAVEL, Geneve	Office Manager
8. Mr. K. NEUMAIER	KUONI TRAVEL, Baden	Manager
9. Mr. D. PALMESINO	WAGON LITS COOK, Lugano	Manager
10. Miss C. VERNET	WAGON LITS COOK, Geneve	Jr. Travel Agent
11. Miss B. WEBER	JACKY MAEDER, Horgen	Travel Agent
12. Mr. P. WIDMER	TRAVELLER, Thalwil	Manager
13. Mr. W. ZURCHER	JELMOLI TRAVEL Dept, Zurich	Manager

LOCAL TOUR ESCORTS: Mrs. Lucette J. Prestegaard and/or
Miss Melissa Valenzuela and/or
Mr. Allan Norlem

BRITISH AIRWAYS TRAVEL AGENTS FAMILIARIZATION TRIP

FROM THE ARABIAN GULF
OCTOBER 25 - 29, 1976

NAMES	AFFILIATIONS
1. MR. MOHAMED ALI	SADDIKMOHD ATTAR CO., JEDDAH
2. MRS. S. M. SHER	SADDIKMOLD ATTAR CO., RIYADAH
3. MR. FERNANDEZ	KANOO TRAVEL, RIYADH
4. MR. E. GILLESPIE	INTERNATIONAL TRAVEL, DHAHRAN
5. MR. GHASSON TAHA	TRANS ORIENT TRAVEL, DOHA
6. MR. A. MAC INTOSH	KANOO TRAVEL, DUBAI
7, MR. YUSUF ABDIN	GALAL TRAVEL AGENCY, BAHRAIN
8. MR. JOHN CHANCK	BRITISH AIRWAY SALES,, BAHRAIN
9. MS. LUCETTE PRESTEGAARD,	YOUR TRAVEL AGENT, CORAL GABLES
10, MR. SARIZ NAKKASH	ALGAITH TRAVEL, ABUDHADI
11.. MR. N. P. SHAH	EMERATES TRAVEL BUREAU, ABUDHADI

Total: 11 participants including the escort Ms. Lucette Prestegaard

EA 858/26 oct miA-oel
EM 267/28 oct ORL-miA

192

YOUR TRAVEL AGENT, INC.
WILLY & LUCETTE PRESTEGAARD
386 MIRACLE MILE, CORAL GABLES, FLORIDA 33134
TEL. (305) 446-8232

BRITISH AIRWAYS TRAVEL AGENTS
FAMILIARIZATION TRIP TO FLORIDA.

F R E N C H G R O U P Nov. 1-6, 1976.

Name	Title	Affiliation
THIRIET, Mr. H.	D.S.	BA N. France
		Tour Leader
LAUBIGNAT, Mrs. H.	Mgr.	Transcar Paris
LEBIGRE, Mrs.	Mgr.	C. I. T. Paris
DELAIRE, Mr.	Gen. Mgr.	Pyramid Voy. Paris
DROUARD, Mrs.	Mgr.	Mondial Tours, Paris
MONTEIL, Mr.	Mgr.	AOV Travel, Paris
LE JEUNE, Miss F.	Mgr.	Ouest-Voyages, Le Mans
SERVAIS, Miss	Mgr.	Gondrand, Paris
UNIA, Miss	Mgr.	Transp. Mondiaux, Paris
DOMINICI, Mr.	Sales Mgr.	Republique Tours, Paris
COMPAGNON, Mrs.	Mgr.	V. V. S. Travel, Erlont/Paris

Accompanying Tour Escorts of "YOUR TRAVEL AGENT, Inc.":

Mrs. Lucette J. Prestegaard, Mr. Allan Norlem, and Miss Melissa
Valenzuela. One of these escorts will be with the group.

YOUR TRAVEL AGENT, INC.
LUCETTE PRESTEGAARD, PRESIDENT
366 MIRACLE MILE, CORAL GABLES, FLORIDA 33134
TEL. (305) 446-8232

BRITISH AIRWAYS TRAVEL AGENTS FAMILIARIZATION TRIP
FROM SWEDEN
November 07 to 13, 1976

PARTICIPANTS	AFFILIATION	TITLE
1. Mr. Ragnar HAGERTH	British Airways, Gothenburg	Sr. Sales Rep. TOUR LEADER
2. Mr. A. GAVATIN	Mgr. Lin Reisebyra, Linkoping	Manager
3. Mr. B. KJALLMAN	Goteborg Travel, Gothenburg	Manager
4. Mr. I. COLLANDER	Swedish American, Gotline	Sales
5. Mr. I. OLOFSSON	Zodiac Travel, Malmo	Sales
6. Mr. P. HOLMBERG	Vingresor, Stockholm	Production Mgr.
7. Miss L. HOLMSTROM	Resevaruhusen, Stockholm	Sales
8. Mr. I. WALLRENDER	Trivselresor, Stockholm	Manager
9. Mr. B. MEHLER	Flygreseryran, Stockholm	Sales
10. To be advised *MR ALLEN NORLEM*	*YOUR TRAVEL AGENT*	

Accompanying Tour Escorts of " YOUR TRAVEL AGENT, INC." :

Mrs. Lucette Prestegaard, Mr. Allam Norlem and Miss Melissa Valenzuela,
one of these escorts will be with the group.

194

YOUR TRAVEL AGENT, INC.
LUCETTE PRESTEGAARD, PRESIDENT
386 MIRACLE MILE, CORAL GABLES, FLORIDA 33134
TEL. (305) 446-8232

BRITISH AIRWAYS TRAVEL AGENTS FAMILIARIZATION GROUP
FROM IRAN
November 14 - 20

Name	Title	Affiliation
1) DASHTBAN, Mr.	Managing Director	Vanguard Travel Agency
2) MOGADAS, Mr.	Director	Persian Gulf Tvl Agency
3) HOVSEPIAN, Mr.	Deputy Mgr. Director	Intra International Tnl Tv:
4) TAROMSARI, Mr.	Tech Director	Airsea Travel Agency
5) MOKHTARANI, Mr.	Manager	Service Tours and Travel
6) ABCARIAN, Mr.	Deputy Mgr. Director	Round the World Travel
7) SIMON, Mr.	Counter Mgr.	Perse Express Agency
8) MINNASIAN, Mr.	Counter Mgr.	Phoenicia Express
9) BALAYAN, Mr.	Counter Mgr.	Samandari Tvl Agency
10) BEHINAIEN, MR.	Counter Mgr.	Mon Voyage Company
11) GHARIBIAN, Mr.	Counter Mgr.	Ahico Tour and Tvl Agency
12) ABDOLIAN, Mr.	Counter Mgr.	Tops Travel
13) CROSS, Mr.	Tour Leader	British Airways, Teheran

Accompanying Tour Escorts of "YOUR TRAVEL AGENT INC.":

Mrs. Lucette Prestegaard, Mr. Allam Norlem, or Miss Melissa
Valenzuela. One of these escorts will be with the group.

195

YOUR TRAVEL AGENT, INC.
LUCETTE PRESTEGAARD, PRESIDENT
386 MIRACLE MILE, CORAL GABLES, FLORIDA 33134
TEL. (305) 446-8232

BRITISH AIRWAYS TRAVEL AGENTS FAMILIARIZATION TRIP
FROM TURKEY
November 20 to 26

Participants	Title	Affiliation
1) SHCIRZA, Mr. F	Sales Officer BA	British Airways, Ista bul
2) ERVARDAR, Mr. F	Owner Director	Knotuar Turizm, Ista bul
3) CULHAN, Mr. A	Manager	Turk Express, Ista bul
4) PIRINCCIOGLU, Mr. F	Owner Director	VIP Travel, Ista bul
5) KAYALIOGLU, Mr. O	Manager	ETI Travel, Istanbul
6) DEUS, Mr. R	Manager	Globtur Travel, Istanbul
7) CELIKKYA, Mr. S	Manager	Tursens Travel, Istanbul
8) SENGOZ, Mr. M	Co-owner Director	Altur Travel, Ankara
9) CAGATAY, Mr. R	Manager	Vander Zee Travel, Istanbul
10) BAYDAR, Mr. S	Owner Director	Babil Travel, Ankara

Accompanying Tour Escorts of "YOUR TRAVEL AGENT, INC.":

Mrs. Lucette J. Prestegaard, Mr. Allan Norlem, and Miss Melissa
Valenzuela. One of these escorts will be with the group.

12/9 EA # 870 = miA/mco Nov 24 ok
12/9 EA # 717 mco/miA Nov 26 ok

YOUR TRAVEL AGENT, INC.
LUCETTE PRESTEGAARD, PRESIDENT
366 MIRACLE MILE, CORAL GABLES, FLORIDA 33134
TEL. (305) 446-8232

BRITISH AIRWAYS TRAVEL AGENTS FAMILIARIZATION TRIP
FROM GREECE
December 4 to 10, 1976

Participants	Title	Affiliation
1)		BA Athens Tour Leader
2) ANASTASOPOULOS,Mr. A	Co-owner	Triaena Travel,Athens
3) APOSTOLAKIS, Mr. S.	Counter Mgr.	American Express,Athens
4) GEORGAKOPOULOU Mr. M	Counter Mgr.	Argo Travel, Athens
5) KALAVRITINOS, Mr. S	Mgr. Tours Depto.	Wagon Lits Cook,Athens
6) KYVERNITIS, Mr. C.	Co-owner	KM Travel, Athens
7) MASTORAKOU, Miss M	Mgr. Tours Depto.	Air Universal Travel, Athens
8) SAUDAN, Miss S.	Planning Marketing Mgr.	Bamaco Inter.Tvl,Athens
9) SKIADAS, Mr. G.	Co-owner	Arian Travel, Athens
10) SPILIOTOPOULOU,Mrs.F.	Co-owner	Diana Travel, Athens
11) VALIANATOS, Mr. G.	Tvl Office Mgr.	Epirotiki Lines, Athens

Accompanying Tour Escorts of "YOUR TRAVEL AGENT, INC.":

Mrs. Lucette Prestegaard, Mr. Allan Norlem, and Miss Melissa Valenzuela. One of these escorts will be with the group.

Dec. 08/76 - EA # 154 miami to orlando
Dec 10/76 EA # 585 orlando to miami

197

Lucette and Allen would take them around South Florida show them the sights and attractions and even had a barbarque for them. I was involved, being good friends with Lucette and Allen, to get the agents up to Disney World. I would arrange to take them into our VIP group room, get them the airline tickets to Orlando and get them complimentary tickets into Disney World. I had the great help of Ed Northcutt and Marilyn (I think), his assistant, who arranged free entrance tickets with the Disney Company.

It was great to met a lot of nice people even if I could not converse with many. We had groups from Greece, Iran, Sweden, Norway, Arab Emirates, Jordan, France, Switzerland, Ireland, Israel, Saudi Arabia, Iraq, Finland, Turkey and Great Britain. Each group was about 15 agents. We helped introduce all these agents to Disney World and never even got a note of thanks from the Disney Company. We also introduced the agents to Eastern Airlines and got the Eastern name spread around in Europe and the Middle East. (See the individual country sheets following).

The strangest group was the Swiss group. I noticed in the VIP room that agents from around Zurich didn't mingle with the agents from around Geneva. I asked Lucette and she said it was that way the whole trip, they didn't even talk to each other. Maybe because the Zurich people spoke Swissadutch and the Geneva agents spoke French.

We were called on to work at the airport once in a while on peak days when the airport needed all the help they could get. It was no problem for me as I had worked at the New York airports for eight years. We normally worked in front of the counter helping people get checked in but once in a while we helped check baggage also. I received a few nice letters from people who were totally confused by the crowds and the problems of getting checked in.

I was also called on to handle some VIPs that needed special arrangements to accomplish their work. I received a few nice letters from them also. I have included a few to show what type of work they were doing. It kept life from getting humdrum.

I would be remiss if I didn't mention a great trip TIA had in 1984 on a barge in France. The trip was originated by Nina Meyer of Vision Travel. She had a contact with Continental Waterways and they agreed to take a group of travel agents on one of their barges in France. Lynn Swanson of Air France chimed in with air space on Air France from New York to Paris, and I contributed the air space from Miami to New York. When we arrived in Paris they had a bus pick us up and we were driven directly to the barge, the "L'Escargot" and got underway at once. The cabins were small but that did not detract from the trip at all.

We were on the Loing Canal, which more or less parallels the Loing River. The routine was to have breakfast then the bus would pick us up and do a sightseeing trip to a near by town. The first was Moret-sur Loing, which is the town Alfred Sisley (impressionist painter) was born and in which he did much of his painting. After that we went back to the barge for lunch, which was always marvelous. After lunch the more energetic of us got our bicycles (there were ten of them) and rode along side the canal until I said it was too bumpy riding there and we should get out on the roads, and we did. We would ride along, find an open bar, stop in for a drink, then ride down to the next lock and wait for the barge, we rode faster than the barge moved.

Diner was always wonderful, complete with a good wine, and after dinner we would walk around a little, then play Trivial Pursuit. Wally Bithorn and I always fought out the end of the game. One day we stopped at a bar and got to talk with the owner. We had some French and he had some

English. He said to come back that night after dinner. He said the captain was a friend of his and would tie up near there.

After we dined, and we did dine, not just eat, we figured we would go over and say hello. We walked thru the small town, after 10:00pm, and everything was closed up tight, and no one was on the streets. We went to the bar and it was closed and I said he said to come back so we knocked on the door and a window on the second floor opened. The owner saw who we were and came down, turned on all the lights, and opened the bar. Some of the local people saw the bar was open and came in and we talked (and drank) until midnight.

The last day we rode 10 miles on the bikes and the only thing that was sore was that upon which we sat. Our Captain was also an aeronaut, in other words he flew a balloon. He had his with him and offered balloon rides for five people at a time at $125.00 each. We had two groups of five go up with him and they loved it. A real fine trip. The farewell dinner was a dress up affaire and the men were told to wear a coat and a tie for the dinner, no one said anything about a shirt ...so I got two guys (Art Horwitz and Preston Locke) and we wore coats and ties. (See picture)

In taking over as sales manager I had the greatest rapport with the travel agents of any of the sales managers in the area. I had the very valuable help of the sales reps and the reservations Executive desk. Nedra Swazy was a big help to me writing numerous letters for me, which were very diversified as I was involved in may things. And when she retired I was lucky enough to get Evelyn North as my secretary and she was also a big help to me. She was a workaholic and pounded out numerous letters on a beat up old typewriter. The agency correspondence was redundant but she had to do them all as originals instead of having a computer or and electronic typewriter. Evelyn typed all the agency corre-spondence, all the brochures and the rooming lists for the fam trips, all the invitations for events, agenda for the meet-ings and events and the monthly Agency News Letter.

One of the things I did was to write a monthly news letter for all the travel agents. The letter was to keep the agents up to date on what was happening at Eastern, new routes, air-planes, fares, promotions and items important in the industry. I received some very nice comments from Russ Ray, Bill Gregg and the travel agents. See a few of the letter and the comments from a few readers. It was not easy finding perti-nent information every month, but I got it done for about eleven or twelve years.

Another fun thing we had was invitations to the opening of new hotels and the arrival of new cruise ships. The compa-nies would invite some of the agents and some of the airline people. Naturally Eastern being the biggest airline in Miami, we were invited to many things. We did not go to all of them but we managed to get to some of the more interesting ones. One I went to was the opening of Bonaventure Coun-try Club way out on State Road 84. It was out there all alone and so far I almost turned around and went home. It was a beautiful affaire with celebrities from Hollywood, CA. There was Dick Patton, Lloyd Bridges and Sonny Bono to name a few. They took my picture with Edie Driest of Esquire Travel and Suzie and Sonny Bono. (See Picture)

Formal Dinner requiring coat and tie. Shirts?

Well, I guess you all know by now but just in case - as of June 8th there will be no 9% commissions paid on any fare. There will only be 7%, 10% or 11% commissions paid. Fortunately all the fares are higher so over all you will have a net gain.

If you are sending your clients to air cooled Canada remember Eastern has an 9:00 a.m. flight to Montreal which will give them a great arrival time, and time to get acquainted with their surroundings in the daylight. We have both ITX fares and excursion fares to Canada both of which require a minimum stay of seven days.

I hope you all are using the new tour ticket, as it can save you time and trouble. By using this ticket, you no longer have to fill out the ATC-4 form which became obsolete on May 20th.

Enclosed are two flyers, one a group package to Cerromar and the other a group package to Dorado Beach. The nice thing about it besides the price is that you earn 11% commission on the group package until September 30 1974. Both hotels can be booked through your Eastern Airlines executive girls. Both are operated by the very dignified Rockresorts so they don't mention that both hotels have plush casinos. There is free shuttle service all day and all night between the two hotels, so if your client loses in one casino he can try his luck in the other.

I don't think too many of you were paying attention when I told you of our great New Orleans commuter service so---WE HAVE GREAT COMMUTER SERVICE TO NEW ORLEANS---y'all hear?

Our new Holiday Inn program is moving right along. I hope you are making two commissions using this service. The only criticism we have heard so far was that all Holiday Inns do not pay commission. Well, if the Inn you have chosen does not pay commission our executive desk girls will so inform you and recommend a hotel in the area that does pay commission. You can't beat that for service.

Also enclosed is our Mexico GIT program with MTA (Mexico Travel Advisers). Note the excellent arrival and departure times in Mexico City. Have you ever told a client he had to get up at 5:00 a.m. to get the flight home? Well, our flight does not leave until 2:00 p.m. - a great improvement.

Larry Green
Manager/Agency Sales

203

HARRIS TRAVEL SERVICE, INC.

November 1, 1977

Mr. Russell Ray
Senior Vice President, Marketing
Eastern Airlines
Post Office Box 787
Miami International Airport
Miami, Florida 33148

Dear Russ:

You might not even be aware, but one of the other hats that I wear is Managing Partner in Harris Travel Service, Inc. In the course of that position, I try to stay current with travel information as supplied by the various carriers.

There is no question in my mind that Eastern Airlines "Agency Update", as written by Larry Green of your organization, is the most succinct, informative, and most importantly, the most entertaining of all those publications.

Since I assume the purpose of such publications is to get the agents to read them, your competitors ought to take a lesson from Larry, both as to his style and his incisive ability to capsulize what is really important in a way an agent can read it with pleasure.

I realize you value Larry highly and he certainly does an excellent job in all of the other functions he performs for you, but I just thought this short note, to tell you how much we appreciate the way he does "Agency Update", would be appreciated.

Very cordially yours,

HARRIS TRAVEL SERVICE, INC.

By: _Marshall_
Marshall M. Harris

MMH/cfy

204

November 8, 1977

Dear Marshall:

Appreciated receiving your compliment on our "Agency
Update" and Larry Green of our Miami sales office. I
fully agree that this publication is one of the best in
the business, and am very pleased that you feel the same
way as a user of this information.

I will pass on your remarks to Larry and Don Noonan
along with my appreciation for their efforts in this area.

Again, thank you for the continued business support.

Sincerely,

Original Signed by
RUSSELL L. RAY, JR.

Russell L. Ray, Jr.

Mr. Marshall S. Harris
Harris Travel Service, Inc.
5846 S. W. 73rd Street
South Miami, Florida 33143

bcc: Messrs. L. Green
            C. B. Gregg
            D. F. Noonan

205

Agency Update EASTERN

Agency Update

EASTERN

Dear Travel Agent:

Now let's see where we were when we last visited with the continuing saga of "As the Stomach Churns." Oh yes, somebody changed a fare!

....Now let's see what happened this month -- we filed to extend the one-way Super Saver fares (Y116) to New York until November 15, 1979.

....We have also filed to eliminate the YE6, and change the YE46 to a different structure effective September 8, 1979. The YE46 will now be 40% off and booked as "B". The YNE46 will be 50% off and booked in "BN".

....The group 20 fare (YG18) will now be a group 10 fare. The tour conductor privilege will now give one for each 20 instead of 40 with a maximum of two. The percentage of discount will remain at 30%.

....The senior citizens fare will be dropped at the same time.

....The fares to San Juan and the Virgin Islands go up on September 7th. The YE63 will permit tour conductors and the YAP fares will also permit tour conductors.

....We received a teletype (the day after they went into effect) saying the fares to the Caribbean went up approximately 7%. The Bahamas fares did not go up but will on September 15th. The ITX fare to NAS will go to $64, to FPO $60.00, however, it will be sweetened a bit by permitting tour conductors starting September 24th.

....We are also proposing to change the one-way Super Savers (YE116) to only two fares instead of four fares. No matter what, the fare still expires November 15th.

Some of you seem to be confused between MAARS and the ITT MARS PLUS system. MAARS was a company formed by the domestic airlines to offer a multi-access reservation system to travel agents. The CAB approved it about 6 weeks ago but refused to extend the anti-trust immunity. The airlines subsequently disbanded the whole concept.

The MARS (single A) system is ITT's multi-access system - it is alive and well and selling strongly around the country. Over 750 agents have already signed up. Some ITT officials feel now that the MAARS system is dead, more airlines will now sign up for the MARS system. It is really the only way for an airline to go to avoid rejects and delays in all airline message centers.

SEP 24 1979

SENIOR ... MARKETING

207

We are having problems with auditors about getting the support for agency discount tickets to the City Ticket Offices on time. We, therefore, will have to have the requests in our office at least eight (8) days in advance of the flight date. After that time, if you need a ticket you will have to bring it to the Sales Office for approval and we will have you ticketed at our 36th Street CTO.

Effective on November 1st, we will start flights to RNO, PHX, TUS and ORF. The majority of these flights will be connections over Atlanta. Reno will be a non-stop from St. Louis.

We have some new exciting brochures and ski manuals that just came out. The reps are starting to take them around. If you do not get yours soon, or need it right away, call your rep and ask for them.

We expect to have a couple of good presentations on skiing in some new areas; do not miss them. These are things you can sell!

Eastern has a good connection with British Airways' Concorde out of New York. Going over you can leave here at 8:00 AM and arrive in London the same day at 9:00 PM. Coming back, the Concorde leaves at 9:15 AM and you can get back to Miami by 1:37 PM the same day! And it is First Class all the way.(Oh, what a commission!)

ITT has just signed up Piedmont Airlines and they can now be accessed through the MARS computer. There are a couple of big international airlines that have reached agreement and will make announcements in the near future.

That's all for now!

                          L. C. Green

P.S. This was written in August, but the original was lost by our Print
      Shop.

Agency Update

EASTERN

May, 1983

Dear Travel Agents:

Another great month (April) has just come to a close and thanks to you all - a very profitable month. Eastern now has much cash in the bank to the consternation of the prophets of doom. There are still a couple of nuts from another airline running around town saying we are going broke. I guess they have nothing good to say about their airline and have to resort to these tactics - very professional.

Here's a new way for you to make a few dollars and maybe some new clients. You can fly school children on round trip same day; short haul, no meal flights (no connections, no stop) ages 5 to 18; minimum 10 and maximum 30 in the group; no Fridays or Sundays.

Book 7 days in advance in B Class fare code BXEC 1083 price only $50.00. We reserve the right to select the flights.

I hope you all realize that we are running nine flights a day to Atlanta - that means any time your customer wants to go. And the connections - flights to and from everywhere in the U.S.

Some other schedule high lights:

- Boston   - 2 non-stop flights a day
- Washington   - 5 non-stop flights a day, 2 with 757's plus one non-stop into Dulles
- Martinique   - only non-stop, 5 days a week
- Freeport   - now 3 non-stops a day
- Houston   - 3 non-stops daily plus one more on Sat. & Sun.
- Jacksonville   - 3 non-stops daily
- Kingston   - 2 non-stops daily
- Los Angeles   - 2 daily non-stops plus the only direct flight to San Diego on flight 503
- London   - Yes, LONDON. Effective July 15 - 3 flights a week until Aug. 1st, then 6 days a week
- New Orleans   - 3 daily non-stops that's plus one
- Chicago   - Most non-stops - 3 daily
- San Francisco   - only daily non-stop
- San Jose,
  Costa Rica   - daily 757 plus an additional flight on Sat. & Sun.
- San Juan   - 3 flights daily

We earn our wings everyday

O.K., did I tell you about the new flight to London?

We are changing out pricing program effective June 1st. We will have the capability of ten classes of service - don't panic we are not going to use them all - at this time.

We are doing away with WEB/L fare bases and will use M/K/Q. The WEB/L fares were all jumbled up in their percent of discount. Now the M will be the highest promotional fare with discounts of 50 to 69% of the Y fare. K will be the intermediate fare discounts of 40 to 59% and Q will be the lowest fare discount of 0 to 39%.

I heard Eastern was flying to London on July 15th.

There are now five airlines offering automated credit card ticketing machines at airports - American, Muse, Continental, Southwest and PSA. Interesting development - they must have a lot of travel agent friends.

We have received a few indications as to what the IRS will do on fringe benefits. First off all, account travel at 50% is eliminated. You received a letter from Paul Anger to that effect. The letter attached a copy of the type of letter that needs to accompany each and every request for a free or discounted ticket. This letter must be on your letterhead (no half sheets or speedy memos). The agency may accrue a tax liability and you must keep records. We will reject any request that does not have the letter. (#2 club, promotional ticket and 75%'s).

Eastern is still one of the few airlines that give you positive space with the 75% discount. That shows Eastern's feelings toward travel agents as opposed to those airlines who feign friendliness, but are not.

Systemone now has 115 hotels in the London area and surprisingly there are some that are still available. We now have 8,500 properties in 3,800 cities and we have another 4,500 coming on line within 30 days. That will be 12,500 hotels for you to book. And remember you get $1.00 per hotel booking regardless of the number booked.

Systemone still remains the #1 seller of computers. We have caught and passed TWA in systems installed (nationwide). There is still someone else selling a foreign computer (foreign to Miami) at a low ball price, however, keep in mind Eastern will match any price that these foreigners give you. Don't fall victim to a high pressure tactic - call us first before signing.

When Mary Ann answers the phone and asks you questions. She is only trying to help you. Many times she can start working on a problem so the account exec can finish it off for you.

210

Whenever we got a new airplane Don Noonan would try to get a fly around for the local agents and commercial accounts. He was able to get one fly around for the L-1011, the 747, and the Air Bus. We did not buy the 747 but rented two from Pan AM. On the fly around we went up around the assembly building at Cape Canaveral and with the Air Bus we went down around Key West. We usually had wine and snacks for our guests.

We even went to New York on a couple of invitations and brought some agents with us. These were usually Saturday to Sunday invitations. We were invited to overnight on Holland America's New Amsterdam and Celebrity's Zenith in New York and made travel agent fam trips out of those two trips. In Miami we were invited to overnight on Royal Caribbean's Nordic Empress.

Eastern used a company in New York run by a man Morris Silver who did sales promotion for Eastern Airlines. He also had other company accounts. Whenever he had a good deal in New York he would call me as he knew I would work with him. Once he had a new hotel, the Berkely Square, opening and the hotel wanted a group of travel agents to stay for two nights, Friday and Saturday, to inspect the hotel. I said sure I would get 18 agents together and bring them to New York. The price of the trip was to be $10.00 and included two nights hotel plus two breakfasts and one dinner. I also had the agents take the Circle Lines cruise around Manhattan Island. This is the best sightseeing trip in New York

We had another trip to New York courtesy of Morris Silver, also for $10.00, where we stayed at the New York Hilton. I took the group over to Studio 54 one night and they threw us out. I guess we did not look the type for their crowd. There was a fire in the hotel on Friday night. We were all sitting in the bar when the firemen came in and used the elevator to get up to the floor with the fire. Some of the guest appeared in their night clothes in the lobby but there was no problem, they put it out and all the guests were OK. Of course we always went to see a show on Broadway on all of these trips. On Sundays some of us would go to he museum of Natural History, which is now a great museum. When I was a kid in New York the museum was the old type with artifacts just displayed in cases or on the walls. Now they have dioramas to display life as it was. We even were invited to have lunch at he Tavern on the Green one time, very nice.

I was friends with Frank Cangelousi, who was the sales manager fro the Plaza Hotel. He used to give me very special weekend rates for travel agents to stay at the Plaza and I used them for weekend fam trips to New York. We would take the agents on the 8:00am flight Friday morning to La Guardia airport and bring them home on the Sunday flight at 5:00pm. I think every sales rep got to take one of these trips. The Plaza was and still is one of the finest hotels in the World. It is on 58th Street and over looks Central Park to the North, a magnificent view. Frank gave me a book about the hotel published on their 75th anniversary. The rate, when they opened in 1903, was $3.50 a room. I know our travel agents, at that time, sent all the customers who could afford it to the Plaza when they went to New York.

Suzie Bono, Larry Green, Edie Driest, Sonny Bono at the opening of Bonaventure Resort in Fort Lauderdale

One of the fun things we got to do was the introduction of new airplanes. When we got our new A-300s we invited the agents and commercial accounts to go with us on a fly around. On this trip we flew down the Keys to Key West and back. We had wine and snacks for those invited and they loved it. In this picture on board the airplane are Barbara Weinkle of Alhambra Travel, Greta Epstein of Travel Etc., Pat Barr of Sheraton Hotels and Larry Green.

Around the end of the70's New York City and New York State got together and started the "I LOVE NEW YORK" programs. They would take some Broadway show people to a city and put on excerpts from a show. Someone (I think it was Joe Lynch) got the deal for Eastern in Miami.

The first one was "Twentieth Century" and we had it at the Coconut Grove Hotel in the basement. It was so so but it helped to establish the vehicle for future productions where were much better.

We brought the "ROCKETTES" down in one of the early years. I got the grand ballroom of the Omni Hotel on Biscayne Blvd for the show. I had all the sales reps dress in tux (men) and ladies in long dresses. They added class to the affaire. (If it needed any more). We had refreshments for the crowd before the show. The "ROCKETTES" were themselves, sensational! We had close to 1000 invites at the show.

The last show I did was "BARNABY" which was at the Sheraton Four Ambassadors. We had the University of Miami singers in the show also. After that Lou Greenwell wanted to do the set up and Don said ok let him do them. Lou used the Knight Center for the shows and served hot dogs, Rueben sandwiches, beer and soda beforehand and then the show. It worked out just fine. We had "Joseph and His Many Colored Dream Coat", "Ain't Misbehaving" and a few I don't remember. The programs helped reinforce Eastern's dominance in the Miami-New York market. (See pictures)

Another thing we had a lot of fun with was the inauguration of new routes. We usually had a big affair at the Omni Hotel (Biscayne Blvd) This was with very good audio visual, usually provided by Elliott Trotta, a display of goods and artifacts from the tourism directors of the country and booths of the wholesalers involved. This was followed by a wonderful buffett and booze. When we got Haiti and Mexico City routes we had both presentations at the same time with each destination having an auditorium to themselves. We had borrowed a big Mexican flag from Wilbert Sanchez and used a cherry picker to hang it way up high. Some how one of our invited guests stole the flag, how they got up there to get the flag I still don't know. Wilbert helped us with many of our Mexican promotions and was the best representative Mexico ever had, and I still owe Wilbert a flag.

Usually on the first flight to go to the new destination one of the sales reps and I would go out to the airport to see the flight off. We usually had a gift for each of the passengers, frequently a coffee mug with the new destination printed on the side. If we had enough mugs we would give each of the crew a mug also and a few of the mechanics that were handling the flight. Since there were only about 200 made for each flight they are probably a scarce item today. I still have seven plus the Continental inaugural to London but some have gotten away from me.

I ♥ NY

This was the "I LOVE NY" program. It was sponsored by the City of NY, the State of NY and Eastern Airlines in Miami. We had the program for many years and it was an excellent promotion. The second or third year we had the Rockettes down for the presentation and they were sensational. We used the large ballroom at the Omni Hotel on Biscayne Blvd. I had all our male sales reps in tux and our lady sales reps in long gowns. We had over 1,000 travel agents and commercial accounts in attendance.

When Don was sales manager he was a member of the Executive Association of Miami, which was the premier business association in Miami. Only one company of each type of business could become a member. All the big corporations in Miami belonged to this association. Eastern was the only airline in the group. After Don was made Regional Sales Director I was designated to be the member. There were two members from each company and Bill Southwick, who was a vice president of Eastern was the second member but he seldom came to the meetings. I went to the meeting every Tuesday morning at 8:00am and often to the visitations at one of the companies locations on Thursday nights. When I decided to take early retirement I called Bill Southwick and told him I was leaving and to turn the meetings over to him but he said I was too late he had already filed for his retirement from Eastern.

I put on the first (of four) big seminars for the Caribbean in April 27, 1976 at the Ramada Hotel on NW 21st Street (new at the time, now torn down). The date was April 27, 1976. We invited (with the help of George Lyall and Arnie Deleo) six Caribbean governments to participate along with Caribbean Holidays, Go Go Tours, Le Beau Tours. Mike Picot also came in as a sponsor for the Holiday Inn of Aruba and the Holiday Inn of Curacao.

The Islands that participated were Aruba, Barbados, Curacao, Antigua, Martinique and St. Maarten. We had Watti Chai for Aruba, Julian Marryshow for Barbados, Raphaelito Hato for Curacao, Lionel Hurst, Edie Hill-Thibou, Yvonne Maginley, and Irma Tomlinson for Antigua, Edmond Jean-Baptiste for Martinique and Arnold Scott for St. Maarten.

I had set the function rooms up so that each island had a room named for them. The presenters stayed in the room and did the presentation six times. The agents moved from room to room according to a schedule. As the agents came in we assigned them to group A thru F. Each session lasted 25 minutes and then the agents had 5 minutes to change rooms. After three sessions we had a coffee break with sodas and pastries. After the six seminars we had a buffet and drinks set up for them. It worked very well but I did realized that I started it too early for travel agents at 1:30pm. The next ones would be later.

Don Noonan, Regional Manager of Passenger Sales and Dennis Shine, Manager of Passenger Sales in Broward County were set up as the hosts as we always included Broward in this type of program since the areas are so close together and most of the Caribbean flights had to originate in Miami. Besides setting up and monitoring the program I also had all the invitations printed and mailed with the help of Evelyn and the Eastern mail room.

The second one I did was in August 17, 1978 at the Sheraton River House as their rooms were all in a line and they had a big ballroom. In fact I guess all the rest and the South American functions were at the Sheraton.

The Islands that participated in the second function were Antigua, Barbados, Haiti, St. Maarten, St Lucia and the U. S. Virgin Islands. We had David Fernandez for Antigua, William Grimm for Barbados, Herman Stephenson for Haiti, Hyacinth James for St Lucia and Ludvig Harrigan for the Virgin Islands. The St Maarten representative canceled out at the last moment and I ended up doing the St. Maarten presentation as I knew the Island well.

We had a third May 17, 1979 with Antigua, Aruba, Barbados, Curacao, Haiti, St Maarten and Trinidad/Tobago. The fourth was on May 13, 1981 with Aruba, the Yucatan, Jamaica, Guatemala, Curacao and Barranquilla.

And when we did the South America seminar by it self (each country had their own room) at the Sheraton River House one it was the biggest of all. We had about 500 agents at that function plus wholesalers and other South American entities. I remember Darius Morgan of Crillon Tours brought up a reed boat from Lake Titicaca to exhibit. Darius runs the hydrofoil boat on Lake Titicaca.

In 1982 I won the salesman of the year award and I was very embarrassed when I went up to receive the plaque. As seen in the picture I am the only one with out a tie. When we checked into the Contemporary Hotel at Disney World the rooms were not ready and they had us put all our bags in a big store room. We were told the bags would be delivered to our rooms. Well the suit bag was delivered but my little bag was not. We looked for it for three days and could not find it. On check out the bag was found, it had been delivered to a room where another person by the name of Green was housed. There were two people in the room and each thought the bag was the other persons.

In 1983 or 4 we had a division sales meeting in Santo Domingo. The division consisted of South Florida, the Caribbean and South America. George Lyall brought in all the sales people. Don Noonan handed out a cup to the South Florida people which says "three quarters of a billion dollars" which is what the South Florida sales people achieved the year before. It was a fine meeting and great to meet all the sales people from all over. George Lyall gave me a nice compliment when he said "I know everything is all right in Miami, I don't get the phone calls I used to get in San Juan, Larry Green takes care of everything."

The meeting went along very well and at the end George asked if there were any problems from the sales reps. There were a few and George noted them. In his report to Russell Ray he listed everything including the complaints. Russ blew his top and wanted to fire George Lyall and Don Noonan. The investigation included a meeting in the library with John Walsh, Russ's assistant, taking notes. I remember Dennis Shine and I were there plus a few others. George and Don were not invited. I somehow became the spokesperson. They wanted to know what the sales reps problems were and I told them.

Eastern Airlines
cordially invites you
to an in-depth
Caribbean Seminar and
Trade Show on

Antigua, Aruba, Barbados,
Curacao, Haiti, Saint Maarten,
Trinidad/Tobago

Tuesday, May 17th, at 4:00 p.m.
Sheraton River House

Refreshments   R.S.V.P.
Door Prizes   Dade 873-2711
Weekends in   Broward 525-3145
these Islands   Palm Beach 655-8345

Welcome to Eastern's Caribbean. You will have six seminars to
attend on the following schedule:

Session I   3:15 PM to 3:40 PM   Session IV 5:05 PM to 5:30 PM
Session II   3:45 PM to 4:10 PM   Session V 5:35 PM to 6:00 PM
Session III   4:15 PM to 4:45 PM   Session VI 6:05 PM to 6:30 PM

Coffee break 4:45 PM to 5:05 PM   Reception 6:45 PM to 8:00 PM

The following representatives will present the seminar:

Antigua   : David Fernandez

Barbados   : William Grimm

Haiti   : Herman Stephenson

St. Maarten   : To be announced

St. Lucia   : Hyacinth James

Virgin Islands   : Ludvig Harrigan

The familiarization trips are designed for working travel agents
only. Outside sales persons may qualify only if they fulfill
CAB regulations which requires a W-2 form or a 1099 form which
shows a minimum salary or salary plus commission paid of 35 hours
x 50 weeks x minimum wage ($2.60 per hour).

Please put only one card in one box. Only one person per office
will be included on each trip. A second person will be waitlisted
and cleared if space opens up in the last week before the trip.

We hope you all learn from these seminars and are better able
to sell the Caribbean to your clients.

April 14, 1976

Mr. Watti Chai
Aruba Tourist Bureau
Oranjestad
Aruba Netherlands, Antilles

Dear Mr. Chai:

We are delighted that the Island of Aruba will be represented
at our Caribbean Seminar to be held on April 27, 1976.

We have selected the Ramada Inn at 3941 N. W. 22nd Street,
(just East of the airport) as the site for the seminars. We
will set up six rooms and assign each tourist board to a
room. The travel agents will be rotated in groups of 20-25
through the six rooms. The seminar schedule will be:

1st	1:30 p.m. - 1:55 p.m.	4th	3:15 p.m. - 3:40 p.m.
2nd	2:00 p.m. - 2:25 p.m.	5th	3:45 p.m. - 4:10 p.m.
3rd	2:30 p.m. - 2:55 p.m.	6th	4:15 p.m. - 4:40 p.m.
Coffee Break		Reception 5 p.m. - 6:30 p.m.	

At the reception we hope to provide details for familiarization
trips to your island.

We need to know if you need any special arrangements; audio-
visual equipment, movie screens, etc.

If you need reservations at the hotel, we will be happy to
make them for you. If you wish us to meet you at the airport,
we will be happy to do so.

Please let us know as soon as possible what your plans are.
If you need to call me in Miami, my phone is 873-2717.

                        Sincerely,

                        L. C. Green
                        Manager Agency Sales

LCG:ncs

bcc: A. Deleo
     F. Calimano

SONTHEIMER AND COMPANY, INC.
445 PARK AVENUE
NEW YORK, N.Y. 10022

(212) 688-8350
OFFICIAL DE REPRESENTATIVES

August 21, 1978

Mr. Larry Green
Eastern Airlines
4890 NW 36th Street
Building 40
Miami, FL 33148

Dear Larry Green:

I understand from Helen Nielsen that you did a splendid job in handling the
St. Maarten presentation at the Eastern seminar last week. I'm just sorry
that we couldn't participate.

A new film on the island is in production. It should be ready by the first
of the year and would be available to you for any future presentations.

If you haven't already mailed back our slide show, I'd appreciate it if you
would do so right away. We have another presentation scheduled up here.

Sincerely,

Janet Myers

JM/db

United States Virgin Islands

Division of Tourism, 100 North Biscayne Boulevard, Suite 904, Miami, Florida 33132 (305) 371-6382

Ludvig E. Harrigan
Regional Director

August 30, 1978

Mr. Lawrence C. Green,
Manager/Agency Sales
EASTERN AIRLINES, INC.
4890 N. W. 36th Street
Miami, Florida 33148

Re: EASTERN AIRLINES CARIBBEAN SEMINAR - Sheraton River House 8/17/78

Dear Mr. Green:

You are to be commended for the excellent planning and execution of the recent Caribbean Seminar.

As a participant, I am thoroughly satisfied that the program was a worthwile vehicle for promoting the Virgin Islands as well as the other Eastern-Caribbean destinations.

Judging from various comments I overheard, the Travel Agents in attendance were also very pleased that their time was well spent in the persuit of a better education on the Caribbean as a fine product for their clients.

We will be happy to participate in any of your future carrier/destination presentations without hesitation.

Best Wishes

Ludvig E. Harrigan

cc: Mr. Paul Auger, Director/Agency and Tour Sales - Eastern Airlines
    Mr. Donald F. Noonan, Manager/Passenger Sales - Eastern Airlines

227

Telephone: 20029
Cable: TOURISM

ANTIGUA

DEPARTMENT OF TOURISM

P. O. Box 363
High Street
St. Johns
Antigua, W. I.

May 12, 1976.

Mr. L.C. Green,
Manager Agency Sales,
Eastern Air Lines Inc.,
4890 N.W. 36th Street,
Miami, Florida 33148.

Dear Mr. Green:

    On behalf of the Antigua representatives who participated in the recent Caribbean Seminar sponsored by Eastern Airlines, I would like to thank you for your personal assistance to our group and at the same time commend you for the excellence of the programme.

    We look forward to your continued co-operation.

       Yours truly,

       Lionel A. Hurst
       Deputy Minister of Tourism

c.c. Mr. B. Cools-Lartigue
     Manager, Eastern Airlines, Antigua.

OVERSEAS OFFICES

U.S.A.	CANADA	ENGLAND
ANTIGUA-BARBUDA INFORMATION OFFICE	ANTIGUA-BARBUDA INFORMATION OFFICE	E.C.T.A.
Suite 931 North	Suite 1104	Room 238/240
101 Park Avenue	21 St. Clair Ave. East	West Block Air Terminal
New York, N. Y. 10017	Toronto, Ontario, Canada	Buckingham Palace Road
Phone (212) 683-1075	Phone (416) 961-3085	London, S.W. 1, England
		Phone 01-730 6221/2

Salesman of the Year award-Paul Auger, George Lyall, Larry Green, Russ Ray

Big South American Fiesta, Larry Green with Joan Gonzales promoting Peru Hotels

First was a question of salary, Sandy Rabb had brought up in the sales meeting her salary. I asked John when a person was promoted to a sales position from an agent position how long was did it take for the position to pay off, money wise. I said two years, five years, how about ten years. I told him Sandy had been a rep for almost ten years and if she had stayed as an agent she would be making more money than she was as sales rep.

Next I took up the fact that sales got no recognition for the what they achieved. I brought up the item in the Falcon, the EASTERN newspaper, where the front page had a city, possibly Charlotte, where the station manager and the airport people were pictured above the caption "xxxxxx breaks boarding record". I said the sales people were the one who broke the boarding record all the airport people did was point the way out the door.

The next point was that a sales rep could not take a client or a big travel agent owner into the Ionosphere Club at the airport. A few of us had purchased cards so we could take our guests in.

We had a few more points and the results were that all the other divisions had the same complaints but did not report them. George was the only one to tell the truth. To Russ's credit Sandy Rabb got a raise within the month and all the sales reps were issued one year Ionosphere Club cards each year.

Somewhere along the line I got the reputation as the man to contact to do a presentation in Miami. I had hotels, airlines and tourist boards contact me and ask if I (Eastern) would help with their presentation. I worked out a deal where we would make the invitations, with Eastern as a co -host, and do the mailing to the travel agents and the other host would pay all the expenses for the presentation. This got Eastern's name out more frequently to the agents and associated Eastern with enterprises not normally connected with Eastern. We got equal billing for the presentation and paid little money as we did so. This stretched our budget so we could do more things.

Some of the people we worked with were Yugoslavia Airlines, Cunard Hotels, Las Vegas Visitors Authority, Barbados Tourist Office, Virgin Islands Tourist Board and others I don't remember. I received some nice letters thanking me for the help they received. I have included a few.

CUNARD
Hotels & Resorts

555 Fifth Avenue, New York, N.Y. 10017
(212) 880-7390

April 7, 1980

Mr. Larry Green
Sales Manager
Eastern Airlines
4890 N. W. 36th Street
Miami, Fla. 33148

Dear Larry:

As always, I very much enjoyed having the opportunity to
meet with you again.

I am enclosing herewith a copy of the Best of Barbados flyer
which, of course, promotes Paradise Beach Hotel in Barbados.
If you feel that your sales people could distribute this,
please let me know and I would, naturally, be delighted to
send a supply on to you.

Naturally, I am delighted that Eastern Airlines will be
running 7 days per week, non-stop service to Barbados and
should you wish to include Paradise Beach Hotel in one of
your inspection trips for your promotional efforts, please
let me know, as I would be delighted to participate with
you.

Yours sincerely,

Marilyn Richardson
General Manager, Sales & Marketing
Cunard Hotels & Resorts

MR/bjr

Irish Tourist Board

Bord Fáilte

590 Fifth Avenue, New York, N.Y. 10036 • Telephone: 212-869-5500 • Telex: 422234

April 14, 1983

LCG,
VERY NICE
& MOST DESERVING
DFy

Mr. Larry Green
Manager Agency & Interline
            Sales
Eastern Airlines
4890 N.W. 36th Street
Miami, FL 33148

Dear Larry,

I would like to take this opportunity to thank
both you and Eastern Airlines for the support
give to the Irish Tourist Board during our recent
Experience Ireland '83 Travel Workshops.

We very much appreciate you providing us with
a special fare for our group from Miami to New York
in March. Our Workshops were a tremendous success
this year and we have received many complimentary
letters regarding same.

Without the support of the airlines we would not
have had such a great success with the Workshops.

Thank you again, Larry, and we look forward to working
with Eastern Airlines again.

Yours sincerely,

Jean Purcell

Jean Purcell
Trade Services Assistant

233

Las Vegas

The American Way To Play

February 17, 1987

Mr. Larry C. Green, CTC
Mgr. Agency Sales
Eastern Airlines
Miami Intl. Airport
Miami, FL 33148

Dear Larry:

Once again, another Miami success thanks to you and Eastern Airlines and we want to thank you for your participation and cooperation. We especially appreciate your help in providing registration people, as well as offering positive space passes to some of the vacation winners.

As I mentioned during the presentation, we're seeing a dramatic increase in passengers from the Miami-Ft. Lauderdale market: 4,677 people a month in 1985 and 11,840 per month in 1986, so 1987 should be even stronger.

No doubt we will see you in January 1988. Thanks again, Larry.

Best regards,

Cam Usher
Tourism Manager

CU:sg

Las Vegas Convention and Visitors Authority • 3150 Paradise Rd., Las Vegas, NV 89109-9096 (702) 733-2323

American Yacht Charters, Inc.
P.O. Box 8740, St. Thomas, U.S. Virgin Islands 00801
Telephone (800) 524-9242/(809) 774-5322
Telex: 3470031

April 19, 1982

Mr. Lawrence C. Green, CTC
Manager/Agency Sales
Eastern Airlines
4890 N.W. 36th Street
Miami, Florida 33148

Dear Mr. Green:

Just a brief note to let you know how much I sincerely appreciate your contribution in sponsoring the two cocktail parties at the ASTA Trade Show last week. Your cooperation in following through with all the necessary details contributed greatly to the success of the showings.

I am pleased to report that we do have several major travel operators who have expressed sincere interest in developing charters for us.

I look forward to a continuing, mutually advantageous relationship with Eastern Airlines.

Sincerely,

Henry H. Blanton
President

HHB:rm
cc: Ms. Heather Lambert
    USVI Department of Tourism

BARBADOS TOURISM AND TRADE CENTRE
199 S. Knowles Avenue, Winter Park, FL 32789

(305) 645-4145

March 25, 1980

Mr. Larry Green
Manager/Agency Sales
Eastern Airlines
4890 N.W. 36th Street
Miami, Florida 33148

Dear Larry,

THANK YOU VERY MUCH!!!

Our recent Best of Barbados presentation tour was a tremendous success
due to the TEAM EFFORT of your team and ours.

I believe a finished presentation is merely the tip of the iceberg . . .
the 90% of the work, such as phone calls, sales calls, follow-up, bags
and boxes, unpack, set up and re-pack, etc., requires the efforts of
many dedicated people working together.

Thank you for your dedication and hard work that you and I know are
what it took to make this Barbados tour the success it was.

I appreciate you and it is my firm desire to work with you to fill your
plane seats to our Gem of the Caribbean . . . Beautiful Barbados.

Have a good day!

Sincerely,

Bill

William H. Grimm
Manager, Sunbelt of the US

WHG/sw

Jamaica❀Hill
Estate Resort and Villas
Port Antonio, Jamaica
P.O. Drawer 330976, Coconut Grove, FL 33133
(305) 661-8846

10 June 1982

Mr. Larry Green
Eastern Airlines
P.O. Box 787
International Airport
Miami, FL 33148

Dear Larry:

Maybe you have heard. Jamaica Hill has been closed. It was a
decision by the board of directors of Klosters Rederi in
Norway. Chilling, isn't it?

I had known for some time we were in difficulty. We were not
able to turn the situation around quickly enough in this
economy. I asked for 90 more days because in that time our
efforts would have shown stronger results. The time was not
granted.

I feel deeply that I haven't been able to give Eastern the
business that was to result from the fam trips we had conducted
together. Apart from business from the agents we had already
taken down, we were just starting the selling programs
involving Eastern with Burdines and Rich's in Georgia and South
Carolina.

Larry, we had the product and the staffing to go with it. What
a shame that people won't be able to enjoy it. Like an unsold
airline seat, once it's gone it's gone.

Now on top of the disappointment, I have to go out and find
what's next for myself.

You have been a great guy to work with, and I hope to do you
some good the next time around. Thanks for everything.

Sincerely,

Herbert L. Hiller

HLH:sm

Managed by New Tourism Headmate, Inc. a Klosters Rederi A/S Company

The one thing that galls me today is the number of people who claimed to have been instrumental in Eastern's success with South America. I did more to get the US travel agents selling Eastern to South America than any other person. Luis Palacio, my buddy, was the man who got the South American travel agents selling to the US. He signed up all the travel agent deals in South America. Yet we hear all sorts of stories, second hand, of people who worked for Eastern taking credit for what we did.

One thing I concentrated on was the leisure business to South America and we did this through the travel agents. All the airlines, including Pan AM, concentrated on the business traveler and the ethnic business.

Very few agents at that time had been to South America. We took hundreds of agents to see what South America was all about via FAM trips. Most liked what they saw and returned home to sell "new" destinations to their clients. We ran many of our own fams, and nearly all of our sales reps got to escort some trips, but it was too much to do and the orders came down from headquarters that a rep could not be away from the office more than 2 days. Since most of the South American trips required 5 days we had to find an alternative. Then came a man, Clarence Simmons who had been a wholesaler in Guatemala, who formed a company called International Travel Directors and he set up trips to most countries in South America at our direction. When we started these trips most of the agents in the US couldn't even spell Quito much less know where it was located.

I was instrumental in setting up South American seminars, as I did for the Caribbean, for travel agents. This was were we invited the South American countries to send up their tourism people to talk about their country. George Lyall was very helpful in getting cooperation from the South American countries. The idea was to have a number of small conference rooms which would hold about 40 people plus have room for audio visual and blackboards. Each room was named for a South American country, such as the Peru Room. We had one or two people from the Ministry of Tourism, from the country the room was dedicated to, to make the presentation to the agents. They were allowed 25 minutes after which we would switch the agents to another room. There were six or seven moves. Halfway thru we had a coffee, soda and Danish break. After all the presentations we had a banquet hall with trade show booths all around the side walls with South American wholesalers, hotels and other South American tourist providers and in the center was all the food and goodies for the travel agents. Chuck Mercurio, who was catering manager for the Sheraton Hotel, out did himself on these food presentations.

One evening at one of these events we had a very odd thing happen. I was checking all the rooms to make sure everyone was set to start on time. I walked into the Ecuador room and there were some 25 agents sitting waiting for the seminar to start but no one else was there. I asked the agents what happened to the Ecuadorian people. The agents told me the Ecuadorians had a video that they couldn't make work so they left. They never told me and here I was with a hole in the middle of the program. I didn't know what to do then I spotted Jim Woodman. Now Jim is a real expert on South America, he knows more about it than anyone I know, except maybe Michelle Shelborne. Besides that he is a most enthusiastic speaker, when he finishes people want to get up and go. I asked Jim if he would speak in the Ecuador room and typical of Jim he said he would be glad to do so. Later some agents told me he had the best seminar. We also had the lady, Michele Shelbourne of LADATCO tours helping us from time to time. And she was another fine lady and who really knows South America.

At one of these events I noticed a man by the name of David Price who was wandering about. I knew the man and I knew he was not a travel agent or supplier but I let him stay anyway. He was walking around the rooms and taking notes. That was a mistake as what he was doing was forming a plan of his own to sell to Eastern. And Eastern bought it. He took everything he learned and presented it as the South American Fiesta. He sold Eastern the idea of bringing in, at Eastern's expense, travel agents from all over the country for the seminars. He made his money by selling booths to the South American suppliers, hotels car rental etc. Here was Eastern paying for what they already owned but since it was just a sales manager who developed it I guess they never considered it. The only one who made money was Mr. Price and I guess he made a pile. It still ticks me off.

After EASTERN went down David Price tried to sell the idea to American. They bought the idea but not David Price. They hired Bill Coleman Associates

One of the other things I did to save money for Eastern was to not let the consolidators into the Miami market. All the South American airlines and Pan Am used consolidators. A consolidator is a company that agrees to direct business to a certain airline for a price. At the time we are talking about a retail travel agent could only make 10% direct from the airlines while the consolidators would pay them 18% or 19%. That meant the airlines had to pay the consolidator 21% or 22% and the consolidator kept 2% or 3% for himself. At that time I had a travel agency advisory committee. I asked them what it would cost Eastern in terms of percentage to have the agent book with Eastern and avoid the consolidators. We agreed the agencies would rather issue the tickets themselves and not go outside their office. This would also have the name of their agency on the ticket and not some company the traveler never heard about. After much discussion we agreed on 16%. We took it to the powers that be and they Oked it but the accounting people were not too pleased as they had to do much of the work by hand not computer. They had us limit the offer to 35 to 40 agents, which was fine as with that we could cover most of the agents who sold South America.

All these programs made the routes good money makers for Eastern so much so that American Airlines paid Eastern $750,000,000.00 for the routes. American followed the same course as Eastern in selling South America and now they dominate South America

Another thing I do not understand about today's retarded airline thinking is how they use wholesalers. If someone came to me to operate a wholesale program I helped them all I could even giving or selling (at a nominal cost) Eastern shells. My thinking was even if they did not produce any business at all they were out promoting Eastern Airlines to a particular destination, using their own time and money, and that could do us nothing but good. They did not tie up any seats and they used their own money to print the brochures with Eastern's name. Today the airlines want to be guaranteed the wholesaler will produce a large amount of business right from the start.

I would help people who wanted to wholesale with Eastern. Following is a brochure I had done to promote business to San Juan. One of our local companies became the general agents for a small cruise line that would leave San Juan and cruise to Barbados stopping over in various islands on the way. Again our print shop people out did themselves. They did the whole brochure including the colors, a four color brochure was too expensive to produce.

To help promote the trip we sent about 20 travel agents down on one trip. Lou Greenwell was the tour conductor. We flew them to San Juan, cruised to Barbados and flew them back to Miami. The Caribbean had the roughest seas in years on the trip to Barbados. Lou Greenwell said only he, Marvin Schwartz and Fred dePue, all who had been in the Navy, were the only ones eating for the first two days. Lou said as they were leaving the port of San Juan the Costa Carla C was in front of them and all of a sudden the ship disappeared, the waves were so rough the ship dropped in a trough and they couldn't see it. He told all the agents they "were in for it".

I flew another group of agents to Barbados and over nighted in Sam Lord's Castle, a Marriott Hotel. We met the other group there and heard their storey. Then we sailed up to San Juan and flew home from there. Our trip to San Juan was so smooth it was like being on a lake. One stop was in St Thomas and it was jammed with ships. There were seven ships on the harbor. Ours and two other ships had to take the passengers to the docks in small boats as there were not enough docking space. The Governor had changed the main street into a one way for the day and the taxi drivers were so mad they went on strike. We were supposed to have lunch at the Virgin Isles Hotel but there was no way to get there.

While we were there a very large aircraft carrier showed up and the Governor petitioned the Captain to stay outside the harbor until the cruise ships left. The Captain did so and as we were leaving the harbor, we were the last ones out, we saw the carrier moving in. It was dark as we left and we could see the line of cruise ships ahead of us, with all their lights on it looked like a highway to San Juan.

In the early 80's was the first time the words "yield management " were used. I can't remember the name of the man in charge for Eastern but in my opinion he was the only man who really knew what it was all about. He was hired away by Piedmont which was too bad for Eastern.

The idea was to place "B" seats (which meant a lower fare from the regular price) on the flights which had a normal low load factor (percentage of seats sold on the airplane). The number of seats varied by the day of the week and the time of the day. This would be an incentive for people to move from the sold out or high load factor flights to the less popular flights and for the customer to save money.

M/S Aquarius winter 1979-80 departure dates and prices.

Day	Port	Arrive	Depart
Sat	San Juan, Puerto Rico		12:00 M
Sun	Gustavia, St. Barthelemy	2:00 PM	6:00 PM
Mon	Fort De France, Martinique	1:30 PM	6:00 PM
Tue	Bridgetown, Barbados	8:00 AM	12:00 M
Wed	St. George, Grenada	3:00 PM	8:00 PM
Thu	Castries, St. Lucia	7:00 AM	11:30 AM
Fri	St. Thomas, Virgin Islands	2:00 PM	7:00 PM
Sat	San Juan, Puerto Rico	7:00 AM	

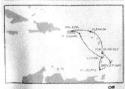

Per passenger rates

		Season*	Off Season**
Group 1	Two bed inside cabin	690	595
Group 2	Two berth outside cabin	795	695
Group 3	Two bed outside cabin (Veda Deck)	925	840
Group 4	Two bed outside cabin (Naxini Deck)	1050	970
Group 5	Two bed outside cabin (Tura Deck)	1150	1040
Group 6	Deluxe 2 bed outside cabin (Luna D.)	1290	1175

*Season dates: Dec. 22, 29, Feb. 2, 9, 16, 23 March 1, April 5
**Off season dates: Jan. 5, 12, 19, 26, March 8, 15, 22, and 29

Prices do not include airfare to San Juan, Puerto Rico and back, and are subject to change without notice. Port taxes, $20.00 per person.

Sample airfare to San Juan, Puerto Rico

From Miami (YATW)	349.20
From Tampa (YA PR)	382.20
From Atlanta	272.20

The Intimate Caribbean Cruise

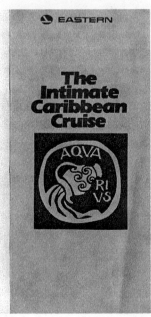

Discover the 2,000-year-old tradition of warm, spontaneous hospitality typical of Hellenic cruising . . . now in the Caribbean.

The sleek and intimate Aquarius, flagship of the Hellenic Mediterranean Lines, was specifically designed for island cruising. And now, after years of cruising the Mediterranean, the Aquarius comes to the Caribbean.

Discover the variety of entertainment available aboard this modern cruiser. When you're not off exploring the wonders of an island paradise or bargaining for native crafts in a tropical market, there's skeet shooting, cinema, sunbathing by our unique movie pool, dining formally at the Captain's table . . . do it all or nothing at all.

At night, the Aquarius is a bit like club-hopping in Europe. After sipping cocktails in our glass-walled pavilion surrounded by the setting sun at sea, and enjoying dinner, you're ready to start experiencing the Aquarius' nightlife. Perhaps dance to the ship's orchestra in the Constellation Lounge . . . or maybe relax in the crescent shaped Belvedere Lounge bar . . . or try the nightclub, where you'll dance to the swinging disco beat on a stainless steel dance floor till dawn . . . unique in the high seas!

Naturally, each stateroom is as comfortable as it is smartly designed. The color schemes selected were inspired by the natural beauty of the islands. All staterooms have 24-hour direct dial telephone service, wall-to-wall carpeting, individually controlled air conditioning and two stereophonic music channels. And you'll be impressed with the ample closet space.

The service is personalized, the way you'd expect it to be on a private yacht. The attitude of the Hellenic crew is that of a host wanting to delight his guests. Don't be surprised if you feel a bit pampered!

Exciting ports of call

San Juan is an old city with quaint shops lining cobblestoned streets, ancient fortresses jutting out to sea, cathedrals and plazas that date back to

antiquity. But it is also a new city with towering buildings and sun-bleached resort hotels. It's a Caribbean city surrounded by beautiful beaches and lush tropical forests. It's a cosmopolitan city.

Gustavia, St. Barthélemy, is a Caribbean paradise just beginning to emerge

as a popular visitor's attraction. Which means it's still largely as unspoiled as it was in the days of the pirates. Tranquility and fabulous beaches is the order of the day here.

Fort-de-France, on the island of Martinique, is like

April in Paris 12 months a year. Its streets are lined with ubiquitous pastry shops, boutiques and balconied houses. But the countryside is pure Caribbean. From its untrammeled tropical forests,

to the top of its volcanic mountains, to its black sand beaches, it's magnifique!

Bridgetown, Barbados, is as British as Martinique is French. You'll see why the minute you enter the harbor. Because you'll see the Harbour Patrol nattily dressed in the colorful garb of Lord Nelson's sailors. In short, the beautiful contrast of things British and things West Indian gives the island its unusual charm.

In St. George, Grenada, you'll find miles of smooth, creamy-white sandy beaches. For swimming, snorkeling, sailing, sunning, and building the best sand castles in the world. Seeing is believing.

Our next port is Castries, in St. Lucia island. Lose yourself in the wide horizons of this Caribbean Eden. Listen to the gentle murmur of the deep blue sea . . . study the soft shapes of clouds etched by the sun against a velvety tropical sky. Set your own tempo on an island that's as casual and effortless as you want to make it. St. Thomas is the shopping center of the is-

lands. The duty-free shops of Charlotte Amalie offer perfumes from France, bone china from England, watches from Switzerland, cameras from Japan, fine linens from Spain, liquor and liqueurs from all over the world, and prices from the good old days.

For reservations or additional information on our 7-day winter cruises, see your travel agent or Eastern Airlines.

PASSENGER LINERS

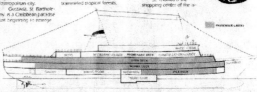

All the smart alecks in the business changed this from "yield management" to "greed management". They jacked up the regular "Y" fare to astronomical heights and added an alphabet soup of discount prices ("H", "K", "L", "M", "N", "P", "S", "T"). There was only a handful of seats in each category. The idea here was to sell the lower price seats first and as the available seats became less and less the price moved up. For the last group booked or people who had to travel it became "sock it to them time". This lead to pricing (an actual fact in 1999) for example to fly from Miami to Washington National round trip in the same week $1100.00 but to fly to Washington International (Dulles) it was only $360.00 for the same days. Of course the airline flying to Washington National had a virtual monopoly on the Miami-Washington route. This micro management of the price is what caused the big airlines to go bankrupt. They change the fares every day all day long.

In 1985 EASTERN started non-stop from Miami to London. I found a red double decker London type bus and rented it for a week. I had three or four of the sales reps dress in English type garb and we toured the agencies announcing EASTERN'S service to London. We had a big production at the Sheraton Riverhouse where all the agents were given derby hats (plastic) with the banned "EASTERN TO LONDON". We had Sandy d'Hemencourt and Dave Lotsey dressed as the King and Queen and had a royal time.

At the inaugural flight I hired a drum and bagpipe band to walk the terminal and end up at the gate the flight was leaving from. We had a castle like facade to walk thru and two people dressed as beefeaters on each side. We got the EASTERN name and the route out to all Miami.

The flight took a while to get going and in 1986 we lost the flight. The official reason was the airplane was not making money. That was not true as I used to get the monthly reports on all the flights from Miami. They were big IBM sheets filled with figures. The most important figures to me were the one that told if the flight made money and if the flight made money fully allocated. Fully allocated meant a portion of all costs maintenance, executive salaries, rents etc were assigned to that flight. In May of that year we made $20,000.00 fully allocated and in June $200,000.00 fully allocated. I think why we really lost the flight was Continental wanted our route and our airplane which was a DC-10 long range. (we bought 3 of them from Alitalia for the South American and the London routes, complete with cappuccino machines).

We also used to get reports every month from the Miami Airport officials. These reports had the number of seats and the number of passenger each airline had for the month. For all the while I was sales manager Eastern had 35% to 37% of the seats out of Miami and we had 43% to 45% of the passengers. That gave us a premium of around 7% to 8% every month.

During the years starting about 1981 there was a major focus on automating travel agencies. All the major airlines got together to build a computer reservations system for the travel agents. It was called MARS for multi access reservations system. In the early stages ITT bought the company and was to develop the system. None of the airlines were supposed to develop their own system. American and United had other ideas. United went to a small company in Tampa called Sabre and paid them one million dollars to build United's agency reservations system, they called Apollo. American went behind them and bought the company for two million dollars and did a good job of getting it ready. Eastern stuck with the MARS system along with Northwest, TWA and Piedmont.

American started to install their Sabre system in large travel agencies. And the race was on. United started putting in their Apollo system and we were trying to place the MARS system. The Sabre system was much better than the MARS system and we could not get ITT to invest enough money to bring it up to par with Sabre. The Sabre system was biased in favor of American and I told the agents that, but the agencies that had the system didn't believe me. It was proven when the government charged American with bias.

This all changed when Eastern came out with System One. This was the best system on the market at that time. We were first to have <u>direct access</u> to other airline participants reservations inventory. In other words using System One an agent could go into the other airlines inventory and see the last seat available. In all the other systems all an agent could see was 4 seats or no seats on other airlines. Furthermore once an airline flight went on sold out status in the other systems it stayed sold out even if seats became available on the flight. That meant the agent would have to call the airline to see if there were one or two seats still open. American said they had direct access but they did not until one or two years later and then they had to called it "total access"since they mislead agents in to thinking Sabre's direct access was the same as System One's direct access.

By the time I retired we had about 90% of the agents in Dade County on System One. We had a great sales team and I believe we had the largest per cent of our agents on System One than any of our other districts. At first we had one person dedicated to System One. First it was Cheryl Parker and she was so very good that System One stole her, then we had Silvia Lopez and then Robert Valido.

The picture following shows the sales team at the SODA presentation October 2, 1984. Jackie Forney and Robert Valido both went to work for Amadeus, which bought System One, for years after Eastern was gone.

If you look at the graph from Travel Weekly of May 2, 1996 you can see the Southern area of the United States still had the highest concentration of System One seven years after Eastern was gone.

Along about 1985 Pan Am had started a travel agents reward program. It started to effect some of our business and as a result I started Eastern's "Number One Club". I wrote it up and sent it to Bill Lush for approval, Bill approved the program with the exception no spouses. I went back to him in favor of the spouse with the rationale that we had many agents here in Miami that will not travel without their spouse particularly our Latin agents. We doubled the points needed for a spouse to travel and Bill, to his credit, approved that. It was a real winner.

ir System

Sodas for SODA subscribers

It was ice cream soda night for more than 400 S. Florida travel agents Oct. 2 as Sales, introduced future SODA subscribers to our automated res system. Above, with Larry Green, left, are, Jim McLaughlin, Sylvia Lopez, Fred Reali, Jackie Forney, Ana Martinez, Adio Roca and David Lotsey. At left, Carol Critten, Robert Vallido and Loren Cain chat.

Everything was fine thru 1985 and then, in my opinion, disaster hit in the form of John Nelson. We had an excellent vice president of sales in Paul Auger when all of sudden for no reason John Nelson was transferred in from accounting. (I understand that there was a reason- he was transferred OUT of accounting). Accountings' gain was our loss. Nelson bided his time for a few months but finally got Paul out of the company. That was a big loss but an even bigger lost was to have Nelson in. Nelson believed everyone over 50 should not be in sales. This despite the fact that Eastern Airlines sales topped all US Airlines for the year of 1985 (for the last time.). See the chart printed in 1995 in Travel Weekly comparing sales in 1995 to 1985.

Regional Distribution of the CRSs

Survey of Small Agents Shows Geographic Spread of Res Systems

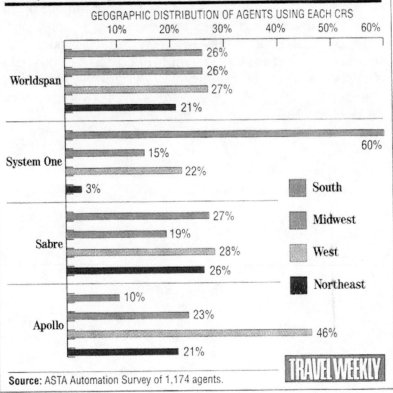

GEOGRAPHIC DISTRIBUTION OF AGENTS USING EACH CRS

Worldspan
- 26%
- 26%
- 27%
- 21%

System One
- 60%
- 15%
- 22%
- 3%

Sabre
- 27%
- 19%
- 28%
- 26%

Apollo
- 10%
- 23%
- 46%
- 21%

Legend:
- South
- Midwest
- West
- Northeast

Source: ASTA Automation Survey of 1,174 agents.

TRAVEL WEEKLY

Changing Fortunes of U.S. Lines

10-Year History of National Market Share for Selected Carriers

AIRLINE	1985	1990	1995
• Delta	11.15%	14.79%	16.51%
• American	11.56	16.04	15.34
• United	10.67	12.72	15.02
• USAir	5.40	12.97	10.84
• Northwest	4.07	8.74	9.14
• Southwest	3.70	4.48	7.94
• Continental	4.52	7.86	7.09
• TWA	5.84	5.41	4.38
• America West	1.44	3.47	3.24
• Alaska	—	1.25	2.17
• ValuJet	—	—	1.07
• Simmons	—	—	0.68
• Hawaiian	0.94	0.57	0.66
• Aloha	0.70	0.53	0.54
• Continental Express	—	—	0.52
• Reno Air	—	—	0.45
• American Trans Air	—	0.04	0.42
• Atlantic Southeast	—	—	0.39
• Kiwi Int'l	—	—	0.37
• Trump Shuttle/Shuttle Inc.	—	0.47	0.34
• Carnival	—	—	0.29
• Midway	—	1.61	0.26
• Tower Air	—	0.03	0.17
• Midwest Express	—	—	0.14
• Frontier	1.92	—	0.09
• Pan Am	3.65	3.07	—
• Eastern	11.70	4.97	—
• Piedmont	5.06	—	—
• Pacific Southwest	2.53	—	—
• Western	3.33	—	—
• Republic	4.88	—	—
• People Express	4.14	—	—
• Total enplanements	357.1	355.2	417.4

Source: Solomon Brothers, from Transportation Department data. Market share is based on enplanements at U.S. airports for U.S. airlines. International enplanements on U.S. airlines are included; foreign flag carriers' enplanements have been excluded.

In my estimation not only did John Nelson not know the airline business he also did not know people. I remember one time a man came to me to block a number of seats for a wholesale program he was doing. He wanted 10 seats on each flight to the Caribbean on Fridays and 10 seats from Cleveland, Detroit, Pittsburgh and a few other cities to connect with the Caribbean flights. I thought it over carefully and told him no. It was not to the benefit of Eastern Airlines. I did not think the man had the ability to fill the seats he wanted. Some how he got around me and got to John Nelson. John Nelson had the group desk block the seats. The group desk was in the reservations office as was the sales office. I knew all the group desk people (Linda Nichols, the supervisor, Jane Taylor, Rita Bromhall, Fran Brodbeck and Alina) and they were great. They told me after three months the man had only sold three seats out of all the seat he blocked. Naturally the program was canceled.

There were also to be a number of age discrimination suits following Nelsons personnel moves in the next few years but I don't know how they came out. Many other people, eased out, were offered so many weeks pay and other incentives to leave. Bill Lindsay in Pittsburgh, Maria Townsend in Hartford, Don Alsup in Nashville, myself in Miami were all people who had their cities in the palm of their hands and were aced out by Nelson. Nelson also aced out my boss, Don Noonan. Don was the regional director and was doing a good job despite the medaling of Nelson with the sales managers. However Don was 60 years old so he had to go. He was offered the sales managers job in Ft Lauderdale (which I guess Nelson didn't think he would take but that covered him with the age discrimination people). Don said no he would just take his severance and pension and leave. Don went on to take the sales managers job for the Palm Beach Visitors and Convention Board and did his usual very good job. We lost some good people who were doing a much better than job, it turned out, than their replacements.

Our sales people had a very good rapport with the travel agents. In a threatened strike a few years earlier many agents called me to say they would volunteer to go to the airport and work the bags for us. That is how well Eastern was thought of by the agents all across the country. When the troubled times came a few years later the new people in the sales jobs did not have the confidence, respect or rapport with the travel agents and most travel agents stopped selling Eastern or sold only a percentage of what they used to sell.

At the end of 1985 Nelson decided to replace me (I was 60 years old and couldn't possibly be any good anymore) with Mary Ann Driggers. She was a smart little lady and a good administrator but she was not a sales person. She told me she did not even want Miami and she wanted a small station and was hoping to get Ft Lauderdale instead. But Nelson in his great ability to do the wrong thing put her in Miami. Mary Ann and I got along very well.

The majority of the travel agents were upset with the switch and let their feelings be known by holding a tremendous reception for me. It was a surprise for me and they got me over to the Sheraton Riverhouse on a ruse. The first indication I had was when I saw an agent wearing a badge that said "We Larry Green". I found they all had on the badges and they had a 20 foot banner behind the dias saying the same thing.

They said there were 320 people that night and they turned down more because of space restrictions. Larry Cafiero was the master of ceremonies and it was held more like a roast. On the dias (the roasters) were Ralph Pastor (who I believe started the affaire), Lou Greenwell, Art Horwitz, Doris Green, Bob Ryan and Wally Bithorn. They took a video of the night and it is priceless to me.

In 1986 the troubles started with the IAM contract. It ended up with Eastern being sold to Frank Lorenzo of Continental Airlines. The blame can be put on both sides labor and management. In my opinion Charlie Bryan was a little ego maniac and the board of directors not much better. Frank Lorenzo took control of Eastern in November 1986.

As it was told to me when the final negations were being made the two sides came to an agreement on all items with the exception that Charlie Bryan insisted that Frank Borman had to go. Frank said he would leave but the board of directors said no they would sell the company first. And they did - they sold us down the river. They looked around for the man who would be worse for the union. They found Frank Lorenzo, who had broken the pilots strike at Continental, and sold to him at the reported price of 600 hundred million dollars. Lorenzo got his money back quickly as he sold the Shuttle service to Donald Trump for a reported 450 million dollars, half on System One, Eastern' computer reservation system, to EDC for 400 million dollars and the South American routes to American Airlines for 750 million dollars. If the reported figures are correct Lorenzo got back 1.6 billion dollars on his investment of 600 million dollars. Plus all the other things he transferred to Continental from Eastern.

In 1987 Eastern and Continental combined their sales forces into Continental-Eastern Sales Incorporated, a separate company but controlled by Vice Presidents from the two companies. They were Jeffery Kreider from Continental and George Brennan from Eastern. Both were vice presidents in Continental-Eastern Sales Incorporated (CESI) but Kreider was the top man. George didn't last very long. I think he decided that the organization was for the birds and resigned to go back to Eastern.

256

Larry's Gala at the Sheraton River House Nov 1985. Seated on the dais are
Bob Ryan, Larry and Wally Bithorn

Mercy Bithorn tries Wally's wig on Larry. Seated are Art Horwitz, Ralph
Pastor, Bob Ryan and Doris Green

257

About that time we were awarded the route from Miami to Madrid. We did all the set up work and even had a big kick-off reception at the Omni Hotel which George Brennan, who was back with Eastern as vice president of sales, presided over. We had wholesalers prepare programs and brochures with the EASTERN name on them and we never started the flight. I don't know the exact reason for not flying but I know I felt very bad because I had talked the wholesalers into producing the brochures. They spent the money and we did not reimburse them for the costs, all the brochures had to be thrown out.

When John Walsh came in as regional sales manager I was transfered to the regional office and named manager of international sales for Continental/Eastern Sales Inc. I worked out a scheme for getting new business class and first class passengers for Continental's London flight. I got together with the sales managers of each Continental city and the travel agent who handled an account that had numerous trips to London. The three of us called on the account and made the proposal to the corporate travel manager. It picked up a goodly number of new customers. After I left Loudres Perez took up where I left off and was very successful with the program so much so Continental made her a sales manager and then regional sales director for Florida.

When we did the Continental festivities for their London flight I was in charge of that also. They wanted a big turn out for the reception and I did not disappoint them. I choose Villa Viscaya for the venue. London sent over the skaters from "Starlight Express" and we had a stage and a canopy for the show. In the gardens we had the refreshments and the food and we had musicians from the University of Miami playing at various places. We printed tickets and gave them out to the agencies and commercial accounts. We gave out 1,400 tickets and that is what we expected. There were guards at the entrance to pick up the tickets but we found a lot of people came in thru the bushes and other places so we ended up with about 2,000 people. We ran out of food and drinks and everything. On leaving we found the police had set up flares in the street to guide the vehicle traffic on Bayshore Drive, the only time I have seen that.

I was given permission to have three inaugural fams to London and we did them up right. I set up one with agents from Miami, one with agents from Ft Lauderdale and one with agents from the rest of the State but most from West Palm Beach. They were not all the same as I could not get the same location for all three trips. For the trip from Miami the banquet was at "Les Ambassadors" a private club which was formerly the Rothchilds residence in London and it was next to the Intercontinental Hotel on Park Lane. I used a beautiful manor house "Dorney Court" in Windsor for the other groups. For these inaugural dinners I had a black tie affair for the Saturday night banquet in London.

When I went over to set up the trips I visited Les Ambassador to set the banquet. On the second floor they had a large room with three Venetian chandlers. They asked how I wanted the tables set up, tables for four, round tables of eight or ten. I said what I really wanted (but not expecting to get it) was one big rectangular table for all 44 guests. They said no problem they could do it and I said OK do it.

Reception at Viscaya for the kickoff of Continental's flight to London 1987. 1st row Robert Valido, Mary Ann Drigers, Clauda Coupet, back row Dick Weisenborn, Cira Talishay, Lourdes Perez, Josie Casanova, Orlando Salazar

Outside and inside sales reps at the reception Nancy Price, Jackie Forney, Cira Talishay, Josie Casanova, Clauda Coupet, Lourdes Perez, Laura Hernandez, Jim McLaughlin and Fred Reali.

The gardens at Villa Viscaya were crowded but most of the guests were on the other side seated in front of the stage to see the Starlight Express begin.

At the reception Jan Hammond, JH Travel Planners, Larry Green and Doris Green, Travel Express.

The trip started with the guests checking in at the group room for refreshments and seat assignment. We sent half over first class and the other business class and switched them on the return. They left on a Thursday and arrived on Friday. We gave them the rest of the day off until 6:00pm. At that time we had cocktails and heavy hors d'oeuvres. After which we took them to the theater to see "For Me and My Girl". The music was based on the "Lambeth Walk" and everybody came out singing and dancing. Next we took them to a late night supper. I remember Joe Vendi asking me "why a black tie affair?" and I said because that was the way I wanted it, they were going to a most prestigious affair and needed to feel good about themselves. When I saw everyone dressed up for the affair I was glad I did as all looked magnificent.

The next day they had the day off until time for dinner. We hired cabs to take the guests to the club and we met in the library for cocktails. The men in their tux and the ladies in their gowns were marvelous. Then came the dinner which was very good. After the dinner some wanted to go next door to a roof top club in the Intercontinental Hotel. It had a name but I don't remember it. I was delayed settling the bill and as I came out of the elevator (lift) the group was coming back from the night club I asked what was the matter and they said they wanted 10 pounds for entrance. I said let me see what I can do. When I walked up to the captain I could see he really wanted to let us in (the agents looked so great they really dressed up the place). I showed him my card and told him they were all travel agents and he said "go right in".

The next day we took the group by bus to Hendley on Themes. There we put them on a boat for a ride up the Themes. It was a beautiful day and a beautiful ride. We got off at a place called Medmenham Abbey for lunch. It was a historical place and was on the banks of the Themes. After which we bused them back to the hotel. That night we had a farewell dinner at "Bakers" and the trip was over except for the ride home. Once again everyone (except me) rode either first class or business class.

Continental had a vice president who was a lawyer. He had sheparded Continental through the Chapter 11 proceedings and as a reward, I guess, he was made vice president of International sales. He knew nothing about sales or international travel and was (in my opinion) a real jackass. Continental had taken over the Eastern route Miami to London and at a meeting of the sales managers I explained how tough the market in Miami was at the time with Pan American and British Airways two well entrenched airlines with all their deals all set up with the travel agencies and commercial accounts and Virgin Atlantic and Laker taking low price customers. After I explained the situation his constructive criticism was "well it better not be that way". He lasted about a year or so and then a man who knew international sales replaced him.

I took early retirement in February 1988, which made 40 years with Eastern Airlines. The main reason I left was the inability to get thing done. If you had a program you wanted to do or need an answer for some problem you would have to wait and wait, I was used to doing things for myself. If you pushed for an answer you got "if you need an answer right now the answer is no".

Travel Agents on board the boat from Henley up the Thames Ernie Stubbs Prudence & Carlos de Gabriel, Michele & Simon Hassine, Paul Besser & wife and Ruth & Sumner Magnet

On the boat Johnnie & Rita Perez, man from Maduro Travel & wife, Howard & Rusty Goodstein and Mary Ann Richter

Travel Agents VIP trip to London 1987. Pictured here at Medmenham Abbey Simon Hassine, Mary Ann Richter, companion and Sergio Barraras

At the Abbey for lunch are Steve Rosen & companion, man from Maduro Travel, Harriett & Art Horwitz, and Barbara Weinkle

Obviously the two companies thought the same as I did and disbanded Continental-Eastern Sales Incorporated in October of 1988. Then came the process of sending the various sales people to either Eastern or Continental. The fortunate people were the people who went with Continental as the people who went with EASTERN all lost their jobs, pensions, health insurance, long term life insurance and their pass privileges. I did not know it at the time but I was lucky to have left early I lost the health insurance and long term life insurance but received my pension and as I had also retired from Continental I received retirees pass privileges on Continental.

Unfortunately when the big strike came, in March of 1989, most of the sales people that had the great rapport with the travel agents and business travelers in 1985 were gone. We probably could have survived the IAM strike but the pilots make a stupid mistake and also walked out. Eastern filed for chapter 11 bankruptcy on March 9, 1989. Eastern came back in the Fall of 1989 with limited service and lasted until the Gulf War. Eastern ceased operations on January 18, 1991 and commenced liquidation of its assets. The agents no longer trusted the people at Eastern and were booking off of Eastern. Forty thousand people lost their jobs, their pensions, their travel privileges and their health insurance and a 5 billion dollar company folded. Thus ended one of the great airlines of our times.

For all the work I did at Eastern Airlines and around the City and County Lew Price, director of Public Relations, presented me the Key to Dade County and then Ben Grenald, Commissioner for the City of Miami Beach, presented me with the Key to Miami Beach.
When I left Eastern I started a company, World Travel Dimensions with Art Horwitz, of Globe Travel, as my partner. The business was operating familiarization trips for travel agents. American, following the course of Eastern, had us operating

FAMs into South America for six and a half years. This got the agents thinking American to South America and American made the most of it and has never let go. They also had us operate to London, Paris, Madrid and Frankfurt.

After six and a half years American made the decision that they needed more seats for their frequent flyers and they stopped the trips we were doing. We tried to get United to permit us to operate trips with them but they had a regressive management and would not give us space. Not long after that United started dropping city after city in South America as they were not carrying enough passengers.

I said before the travel agent FAM trips were the way to get the travel agent selling your airline and your destinations. I set up trips that were not just for one sales district but the sales manger in any city could book their agents into the trips. Many small cities could not get enough agents together to operate a trip but this way their agents could experience our destinations.

One of the nice things for me was to be remembered as Mr Eastern Airlines in Miami. Ten years after Eastern left us and thirteen years after I retired people still remember me, for example in December 2001 a lady walking behind me said "is that Eastern airlines walking in front of me". I turned around thinking I must know who it was but the lady said "you don't know me but I am Cynthia Fletcher, I was a travel agent and I remember all the good things you did with Eastern Airlines."

That made all the hard work I did for Eastern well worth while.

Left is the Key to Dade County, on the right is the Key to the City of Miami
Beach. They were awarded to me at different times for tourist services to the area